The Pain in Pleasure

The Pain in Pleasure

Lawrence Bolar

The Pain in Pleasure
Lawrence Bolar

Published By:
KPG Book Publishers
(a division of Kingdom Publishing Group, Inc.)
P.O. Box 3273, Richmond, VA 23228
www.kingdompublishing.org

Library of Congress
© 2011 by Lawrence Bolar

ISBN 13: 978-0-9831452-2-6

www.lawrencebolar.com

Cover design: Virgil Brown,
Delmar Photography and Graphic Design

All Rights Reserved.
No part of this book may be reproduced.
This book or parts thereof may not be
reproduced in any form, without written
permission of the author except as provided by
the United States of America copyright law.

Printed in the United States of America.

VISION

The vision for "The Pain in Pleasure" is to create a resource that promotes the Building and Edification of the Kingdom of God. This resource will educate, inspire and transform the minds of all of God's people.

MISSION

The purpose for "The Pain in Pleasure" is to cultivate accurate and relevant real-life analogies along with God's principles. These analogies are actual occurrences that have caused Christians and non-Christians to lose their position in God. The main objective is to stimulate each reader's thoughts, spiritually and naturally, to change.

FOREWORDS

Apostle Elaine Johnson

"God created each of us with a free will. If not used according to His word, we will find ourselves in situations that are not necessarily God's will for our lives. In this place we live beneath the copious life Jesus shed His blood for. Lawrence Bolar has given us some heart-searching things to consider as he has poured out his life experiences and heart matters to us. His unfastened release of this time sensitive subject, "The Pain in Pleasure," will allow many to understand why they have lived a life—making the same mistakes over and over again"

Yvette Hawkins

Wow! I just finished reading Lawrence Bolar's third book, "The Pain in Pleasure" and all I can say is, wow! I am so pleased with the author and I'm impressed with how he has allowed the Lord to use his painful situations to minister to others. In this book, the author uses analogies of what appears to be pleasurable moments that, in fact, affect others in such painful ways. He then gives you scriptural backup that really makes you stop and think. It is a must-have book that deals with real life situations, just as his first book, "Nothing Substitutes Time." When you look at the title, you might wonder, "How is it possible to have pain in what appears to be pleasure?" Well, he answers that in his book by giving you different real life scenarios, and the affect they may have on others. Often times in life, we make decisions without thinking of how they might affect others. As he poured out his heart in his first book, and shared his personal experiences of growing up without his biological father, he has done it again by sharing different analogies of how choosing a temporary pleasure can have a long-lasting, painful affect on others.

I work in a school district in El Cerrito, California and, believe me, every day I see the "Pain in Pleasure." The selfish desires of man/woman to have temporary pleasures are affecting our children every day. I know it was fun or good and may have even seemed like it was right at the time, but has anyone considered the affect it would have on our children? Does anyone care? Here is an example: there is a young girl about 11 years old that has been forced to grow up ahead of her time because mom chose temporary pleasures that is causing her daughter much pain. Mom is having fun, making foolish decisions to have unprotected sex with men which resulted in her having several baby daddies. Is this affecting the mother? Why does she get to continue to have pleasure while her 11 year old daughter is forced to be the mother of several younger siblings? This girl comes to school angry at the world because she is not allowed to be a kid and is forced to be an adult at home. By the time she makes it to school, she doesn't know how to switch roles back to being a child. Therefore, every time an adult tells her something she doesn't like, she becomes unbelievably disrespectful. You know, she sometimes reminds me of me, because I had to take care of my younger cousins because at the time their mother chose to drink alcohol excessively. Although, I feel like I can help her, she is so angry that she won't let anyone in. I have no regrets; I like this author, chose to turn negative situations into positive ones so that we can reach out and help others. I am pleading with you, just as the author is in this book when he gives you many different analogies of how ones pleasures can cause extreme pain on others, to stop and start thinking about someone other than yourself. Stop and think before you make decisions that can traumatically affect others. You must read this book and see how the Lord has given this young man insight that exposes the tactics and schemes of the enemy. It is an eye-opener, one that would provoke positive change. What I like most is he not only has the problem, but through the guidance of the Holy Spirit, he gives you life-changing solutions. Don't allow the selfish desires of the flesh to have temporary pleasures cause you to continuously inflict pain on others. It is not too late to be set free from your past pains!

ACKNOWLEDGEMENTS

This book is dedicated to my Lord and Savior, Jesus Christ, and all the men and women who have encouraged or deposited wisdom into my life. Johnnie Mae Myers (Nanny), my loving grandmother; my parents, Jerry & Debra Underwood; Rev. Ray & Karlyn Smith; Apostle Elaine Johnson, my spiritual mother who has taught me how to apply the word of God through her example. Rev. Leslie J. Blakely for giving me the foundation of God's word; Pastor Vernon and Betty Sue Robinson, Charles II, Yvette & Charles III Hawkins, Pastor Donald Berry, Pastor Van & Casey Bolden, Pastor Lewis Thomas, Pastor Joey Marks, Delmar Photography for a great cover; Jesus Way Fellowship Center family, and RaShawn, my beautiful wife, for all the love and support in making it possible to publish my third book. Thank you to my wonderful children, Lauren and Christian. Thank you to my sisters, Scerina and Yvette, my brothers, Carlos, Mike, Terry, Wayne, and Timothy. Thank you to my entire family, all my friends, supporters and a special thanks to my readers. I also extend special thanks to: Elder Frank Carpenter, Associate Pastor Joann Carpenter, Elder Melvin Jones, Evangelist Terrie Evans, Evangelist Edward Thomas, Evangelist Loresa Sanders, Prophetess Faye Knight, Minister Elvia Deering, Minister Patsy Passmore, Deaconess Sandra May, and Deacon Phillip Sanders. Lastly, a special thanks to Ray and Cassandra Smith, Larry Brown, L J Brown Enterprises, LLC., the models on the book cover: Fatimah Myrick and Tawanna Wynn, Darrell Bullock, Brother's Keepers Ministries, and Reverend Willie McKind for the inspiration of my title, "The Pain in Pleasure."

CONFIRMATION

The following persons confirmed
"The Pain in Pleasure" as a literary work
that is sound in the word of God:

Apostle Elaine Johnson

Associate Pastor Joann Carpenter

Prophetess A. Faye Knight

Yvette Mechelle Hawkins

TABLE OF CONTENTS

Chapter 1: Introduction 17

Chapter 2: The Pain Behind The Pleasure 21

Chapter 3: Bound By Pleasure 31
    1. Lust.. 36
    2 The Things Boys Talk About 38
        A. Product of Your Environment
        B. 1st Graders Planning to have Sex
    3. Proper Rules of Engagement.. 44
    4. First Love Blues 47
    5. Early Exposure to Sex... 54

Chapter 4: The Pleasures of Life Analogies, Part I 61
    1. Who Is the Baby's Daddy? 62
    2 The Simple Lie... 72
    3. David and Melissa.. 76
    4. My Story, Your Story, The God's Honest Truth........ 84
    5. Your Pleasure, Their Pain 89

Chapter 5: The Pleasures of Life Analogies, Part II 93
    1. Playing the Game 94
    2. Two Best Friends, One Girl 94
    3. Two Women, One Man 95
    4. Caught Up With a Booty Call 97
    5. Who's Got Game? 102
    6. The Gym Hook-Up 103
    7. Friends to the End 108

Chapter 6: Spiritually Blinded by Pleasures 115
    1. *The Dirty Deacon* 116
    2. *Pastor Stan* 122

Chapter 7: The Pains of Pleasure 129
    1.   *When the One You Love*
        Don't Love You Back 130
    2. *Unequally yoked* 131

Chapter 8: Theory vs. Scripture 141
    Spiritual Inventory Aptitude Test 169

Chapter 9: The Purpose and Power
              of the Blood of Christ 171

Scripture References 187

About the Author 201

CHAPTER 1

Introduction

Introduction to The Pain in Pleasure

"The Pain in Pleasure" is a book about the pleasures of life that we enjoy that have lasting effects on our lives. This book is filled with lots of true and dramatic events to provoke your thoughts and give you the opportunity to view the choices you make differently. Some of the subject matter is adult in nature. However, not explicit by any means and can be read by all ages. The names in this book have been altered for private and personal regards. This book is filled with shocking analogies backed by scriptural references and biblical principles that follow them. My main purpose for writing this book is to encourage each reader to personally view their choices in life and to effectively analyze the decisions they have made, and will make, in the future. Our world today consists of many different challenges that we must face as Christians and non-Christians. I believe the Apostle Paul summed up "The Pain in Pleasure" best in Romans 7:14-25 when he said, " *We know that the Law is spiritual; but I am a creature of the flesh [carnal, unspiritual], having been* sold into slavery under [the control of] sin. For I do not understand my own actions [I am baffled, bewildered]. I do not practice or accomplish what I wish, but I do the very thing that I loathe which my moral instinct condemns].

Now if I do [habitually] what is contrary to my desire, [that means that] I acknowledge and agree that the Law is good (morally excellent) and that I take sides with it.

However, it is no longer I who do the deed, but the sin [principle] which is at home in me and has possession of me.

For I know that nothing good dwells within me, that is, in my flesh. I can will what is right, but I cannot perform it. [I have the intention and urge to do what is right, but no power to carry it out.]

For I fail to practice the good deeds I desire to do, but the evil deeds that I do not desire to do are what I am [ever] doing.

Now if I do what I do not desire to do, it is no longer I doing it [it is not myself that acts], but the sin [principle] which dwells within me fixed and operating in my soul].

So I find it to be a law (rule of action of my being) that when I want to do what is right and good, evil is ever present with me and I am subject to its insistent demands.

For I endorse and delight in the Law of God in my inmost self [with my new nature].

The Pain In Pleasure

But I discern in my bodily members in the sensitive appetites and wills of the flesh] a different law (rule of action) at war against the law of my mind (my reason) and making me a prisoner to the law of sin that dwells in my bodily organs in the sensitive appetites and wills of the flesh].

O unhappy and pitiable and wretched man that I am! Who will release and deliver me from [the shackles of] this body of death?

O thank God! [He will!] Through Jesus Christ (the Anointed One) our Lord! So then indeed I, of myself with the mind and heart, serve the Law of God, but with the flesh the law of sin.

The goal of "The Pain in Pleasure" is to convey to the reader that pleasures cannot only bring future pain, but can also affect families and loved ones. God has inspired me to write this book for the inspiration of others. It is my prayer that the information, analogies, and scriptural insights will provoke your every thought.

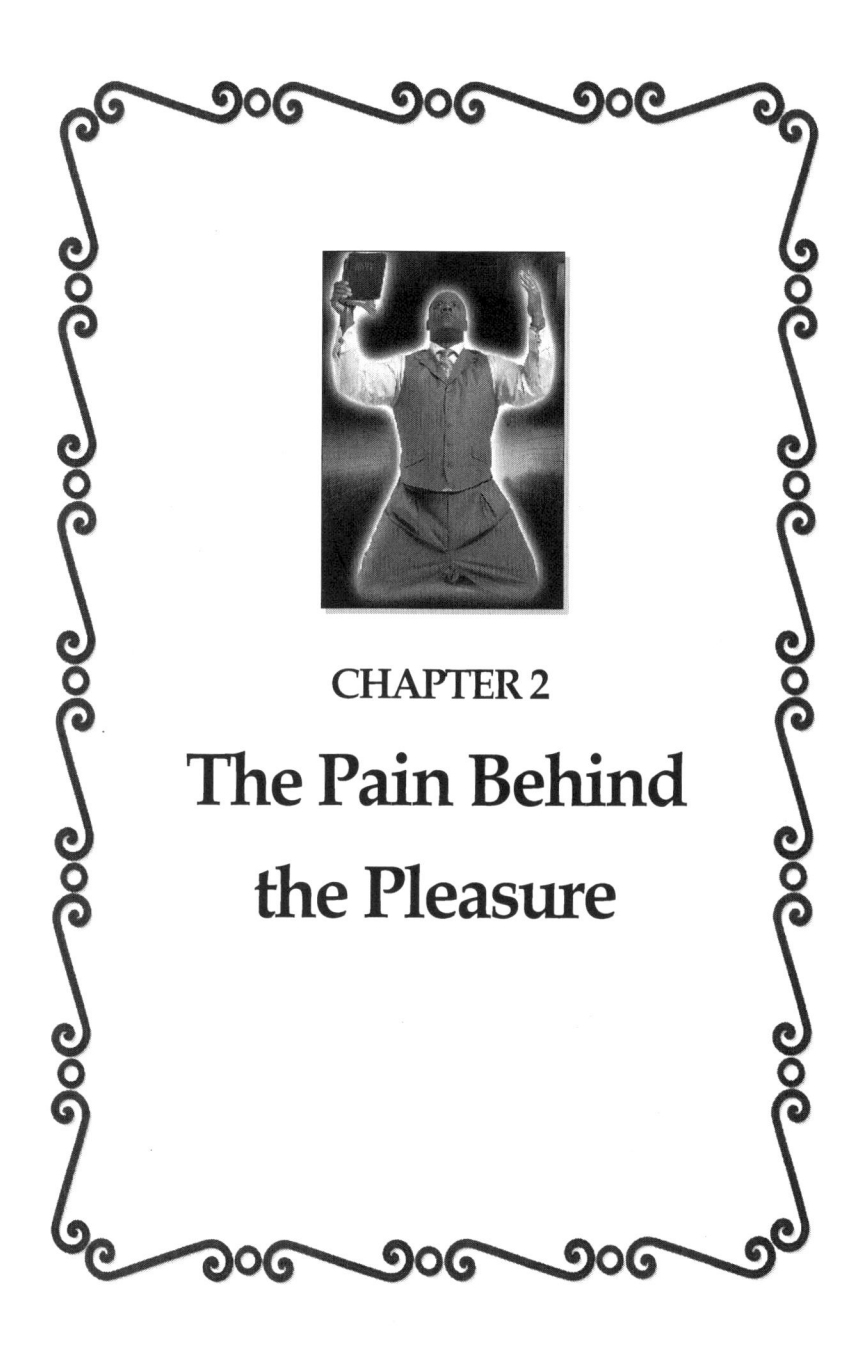

CHAPTER 2
The Pain Behind the Pleasure

The Pain Behind the Pleasure

Why is it so tempting to love pleasure rather than God? Pleasure is something that we can control; God cannot be controlled. Most pleasures can be obtained easily; love for God requires effort and sometimes sacrifice. Pleasure benefits us now; the benefits of loving God are often in the future. Pleasure has a narcotic effect; it takes our minds off ourselves and our problems. Love for God reminds us of our needs and responsibilities. Pleasure cooperates with pride. It makes us feel good when we look good in the eyes of others. To love God we must lay aside our pride and accomplishments. Have you chosen to love pleasure, or to love God? How do you know?

The pain behind pleasure is often overlooked by most people. Pleasure often appears to overshadow the pain. What I want you to see is the true picture behind most pleasures. My intent is to reflect upon bible-based principles, the scriptures, observations and some personal experiences. Following a life of pleasure and giving in to every sensual desire can lead to slavery. Many people think freedom consists of doing whatever they want. What they do not recognize is that this path can lead to a slavish addiction to sensual gratification. A person is no longer free but becomes a slave to what his or her body dictates. Christ frees us from the control and desires of sin. Have you been released? The Apostle Paul summarizes what Christ does for us when He saves us. We move from a life full of sin to one where we are led by God's Holy Spirit. All our sins, not merely some, are washed away by the blood of Jesus. This washing refers to the water baptism, which is a sign of salvation. In becoming a Christian, the believer acknowledges Christ as Lord and recognizes Christ's saving grace. We gain eternal life with all its treasures through His grace. We have a new life we now live, through the Holy Spirit, as He continually renews our heart. None of this occurs because we earned or deserved it; it is the gift of God.

The Pain in Pleasure is birthed out of a life of pleasures, sensual desires, and the refusal to allow God's gift of the Holy Spirit to fully operate in us. By clearly defining what Webster says about pain and pleasure, I can

The Pain In Pleasure

assure every reader that this story will take you on the right journey toward exploring your inner desires.

Pain is an unpleasant sensation occurring in varying degrees of severity as a consequence of injury, disease, or emotional disorder. Most of the pain discussed will rotate around emotional disorders.

Pleasure is an enjoyable sensation or emotion: a source of enjoyment, gratification, or delight.

When most people think of pain, the average person will likely say, "I don't like going through or feeling any type of pain." Pain is often attributed to being negative or bad, but this isn't always the case. Some pain is actually good for you. The good comes from the hurt you feel as a result of doing something that caused you pain.

For example, trials that people go through often cause some type of pain. Normally, when some sort of stimulus is applied to a particular behavior, it will be stored in our long term memory. For example, if you are speeding down the highway and you receive a speeding ticket, wherever you received that ticket, subconsciously, you slowed down. I learned, based on my teaching of the word of God, that trials come to make you stronger. That's only if the pain you experienced in the trial helped. Prayerfully, it will also serve to prevent you from doing the same action again.

Pleasure, on the other hand, is altogether different. Most people will say they enjoy experiencing pleasure and they go out of their way to experience it even if it costs them everything.

The lesson learned here is to get every reader to evaluate their pleasures in life. I'm not saying that we shouldn't have pleasures in life but what I am saying is, we should evaluate them closely. We also should examine God's word to see what it says about our pleasures. Our minds should ponder over the hidden damage that we expose ourselves to without fully understanding the impact of what we are doing. Satan is the god of this world. His work in the earth is to deceive. He has blinded those who don't believe in Christ. The allure of money, power and pleasure blinds people to the light of Christ's Good News. Those who reject Christ and prefer their own pursuits have unknowingly made Satan their god.

The Pain In Pleasure

2 Corinthians 4:4: "In whom the god of this world hath blinded the minds of them which believe not, lest the light of the glorious gospel of Christ, who is the image of God, should shine unto them."

There is a way that seems right unto man but the way there of is destruction. The journey to destruction begins at a very early age. Most children must have boundaries set concerning what they can and cannot have. This is a very complex statement, "what I can have and what is actually good for me." For parents dealing with this, it is often viewed from a different perspective but how a person receives and comprehends it is quite common among most people. For example, a concerned parent will often try to prevent their children from consuming too much candy or sweets because it could cause cavities and obesity. This is based on the child's level of understanding until cause and effect comes into play. Because I didn't listen to the warning or the wise instructions from my loving parent, about not eating all of the sweets or over indulging, I'm now feeling the pain of a severe toothache. I should have been obedient to the voice of my loving father and took heed to the warning. This Is a clear example of how we override the Holy Spirit. The problem is I wanted to do what made me feel good like eat all the chocolate I could get my hands on regardless of being disobedient to my father's advice. This example appears to be harmless but disobedience on any level has consequences attached to it. This type of wrong thinking can potentially open doors for the enemy of our soul to come in to support our disobedience. The enemy immediately recognizes our disobedience to God and works to convince us to follow after ungodly pleasures that will eventually cause pain.

As adults, we often think about what we want, what we need, and what is best for us without any real regard for how it will affect our family. Take smoking for example: on the pack of cigarettes it clearly states "hazardous to your health," but the tobacco industry is one of the largest and most consistent industries in the world today. This is a direct indication of just how much people listen to warnings. Parents often continue to smoke around their children regardless of the warning on the

The Pain In Pleasure

cigarette pack or the affects of second hand smoke. See how pleasures somehow just seem to push right past what you know to be harmful to your children? Choices in life are so important that we must seek God for the wisdom to make Godly choices. Our choices often reveal our true character. Let's view a spiritual example such as the choices that Lot made that ultimately affected his entire household.

Lot took the best share of the land even though it meant living near Sodom, a city known for its sin. The question Lot should have asked himself, as well as God, is "Can I really live in this city without me and my entire house being ultimately affected?" Lot was greedy. He wanted the best for himself, without thinking about his uncle Abram's needs or what was fair. Does this sound familiar to you? Does this sound like something you would have done or that someone you know would have done? The story ends with Lot's family barely escaping the city before God destroyed it with fire. Lot still ended up losing his wife in the process of her own disobedience to God. The only reason he and his daughters survived is because the uncle he thought he was getting over on went before God on his behalf.

Life presents a series of choices. We, too, can choose the best while ignoring the needs and feelings of others. But this kind of choice, as Lot's life shows, leads to problems. When we stop making choices in God's direction, our only option is to make choices in the wrong direction. Have you chosen to live in Sodom? Even though you think you're strong enough to resist the temptations, other members of your family may not be. Lot looked at good pastures and available water which looked like a wise choice based on what was pleasing to his eyes. The outcome showed that his choice wasn't good for him or his family. Our God is Alpha and Omega. He knows the beginning and the end. Sometimes we can't see past our desires. It is like the famous statement, "You can't see the forest for the trees."

One of the most difficult things to get people to understand is that the inner desires we have are often driven by lust. Lust comes in various forms not just sexual. It is the flesh nature and we as humans have to learn how

The Pain In Pleasure

to depend on God's word to maintain control of it or it will consume us. Our flesh nature, based on what the bible tells us, is weak and full of ungodly sin, "the flesh and the spirit is at constant war against one another." As you continue to read "The Pain in Pleasure," you will see just how much war is going on within you.

CHAPTER 3
Bound by Pleasure

Bound by Pleasure

Bound by Pleasure is the first chapter of this book that addresses strongholds. This chapter will give every reader the opportunity to see just where I'm going with this book and to help them decide if they want to continue reading it or not. Please review this scripture for the powerful intent that God wants to reveal.

2 Corinthians 10:3-5 (New International Version)

3 For though we live in the world, we do not wage war as the world does. **4** The weapons we fight with are not the weapons of the world. On the contrary, they have divine power to demolish strongholds. **5** We demolish arguments and every pretension that sets itself up against the knowledge of God, and we take captive every thought to make it obedient to Christ.

This book is extremely important and I believe that, by the grace of God, it will impact the lives of all who read it. This chapter will also focus on Romans 6:23, "For the wages of sin is death, but the gift of God is eternal life in Christ Jesus our Lord."

To be bound literally means to be held captive by something or someone. To be bound by pleasure appears to be, and actually sounds like, it's a good thing. Who doesn't want to be bound by something they enjoy doing? For example, if you enjoy eating chocolate and you have the opportunity to eat chocolate all day and as often as you would like to, then what do you think is going to happen to your teeth?

Pleasure for some people is just what you think; it's about making them feel good. Feeling good often comes with a high price. A person is a slave to whatever controls him or her. Many believe that freedom means doing anything we want. But no one is completely free doing what he or she wants. I have seen lust drive people so far that it literally controls them. The control comes in if we refuse to follow God; we end up following our own sinful desires and become enslaved to what our body wants. If we submit our lives to Christ, He will free us from the slavery of sin. Christ frees us to serve Him. This is a freedom that results in our ultimate good.

The Pain In Pleasure

How do I become bound by pleasure? The bible teaches that in the last days men would become lovers of themselves. Individuals can become bound by pleasure by allowing the sins they lust after to take complete control of their lives. In other words, we would be so consumed with making sure that we please ourselves through whatever means that in the end, we will be controlled by sin. This often means by any means necessary or whatever it takes to get what I want, I'm willing to pay the price to have it. The price comes with a price tag that we often feel or believe that we can afford, but in the end we're trapped.

I believe that when people are bound by sin and it is generational or something that they have been suffering with long term, it's a major battle. In fact, it's a major war going on within the heart of that individual. To be bound by sin means we have already been sentenced to death and we're just waiting on the day of execution. Christ died for the sins of the world so that we would have a way of escape. What happens when we don't want to be set free? As children of the most high God, we have a right to be free but it's a choice each of us has to decide for ourselves. God is a gentleman and will not superimpose Himself or His spirit upon any man.

This all sounds easy, doesn't it? But, if it were that easy, I wouldn't have compared it to a war going on. The war is going on in the mind of a person when he knows to do right, but chooses not to do it. The war intensifies when God's word says, "If you love Me you will follow Me and keep my commandments." However, because our flesh has ruling authority over our actions, the Holy Spirit has been rendered powerless by our lack of faith, trust in God and His word. God created us all with the gift of free will and because of this free will we can choose not to submit to the Holy Spirit. When we chose to refuse the Holy Spirit, our flesh takes complete control. Through "The Pain in Pleasure," you will have the opportunity to review many eye-opening analogies. The analogies are designed to stimulate your thoughts to the point of change. This first analogy about the controlling power of lust will give you a description of how that happens.

The Pain In Pleasure

Analogy: **Lust**

Here we have a Christian man following after Christ but he has a slight problem with his flesh. The brother loves God, but doesn't really understand the importance of having a victorious life with Christ Jesus. This victorious life with Christ should give him the ability to overcome sin and his lustful desires. The Holy Scriptures teach us that, "We can do all things through Christ Jesus who strengthens us." The reality for him is he believes that he has tried to overcome this problem through various ways but with little to no success. This lack of success has discouraged him to no end, so he feels that there is no hope for him to ever overcome this major obstacle in his life.

This Christian man appears to know God's word and he believes that he follows it to the best of his ability in all but this one area of his life. This man has spent a large portion of his young adult life in the church, and he knows in his heart that he needs to make a drastic change in his life so that God may be pleased with his Christian walk. In fact, he knows that he must make a change or he's going to die. However, lustful desires happen to be his weakness. He has been allowing this spirit of lust to be his driving force and even though he appears to think that he loves God with his whole heart, he continues to find himself fornicating and lusting after women. He believes in his heart that he has fought the good fight of faith. The reality of it all is he just loves sleeping with women and doesn't really want to commit to marriage. The man has been saved by the blood of Jesus, however he can't overcome this dreadful sin.

Lesson learned:

Remember in the beginning of the book when the Apostle Paul says in Romans, "I will to do what is right but I can't perform it"? The young man wants to do right and has a will to do right but he can't perform it. The truth is that there are demonic forces that work against our true purpose. This is another example of pain in pleasure, the act of feeling good but the end result is death. This death isn't always physical but may be a spiritual death, which is a complete separation from God. This type of death is sometimes hard to relate to or understand because most people cannot believe that a loving God will put them to death in the spirit. People often find it difficult to relate to things of the spiritual realm.

~ ~ ~ ~ ~ ~ ~ ~ ~ ~

Analogy: The Things Boys Talk About

This whole experience of pain in pleasure can start as early as 5 or 6 years of age. I relate this back to 1st grade, my earliest remembrance of talking about having sex. Yes, I said talking about having sex at this age. This time frame for me was in the year of 1976. I know you're probably wondering how in the world was somebody this age, in the mid 70's, thinking or talking about sex? This was during the time when there wasn't much exposure to sex like it is today. Today, sex is everywhere. In schools, on the TV, the computer, etc. During this time, the shows were black and white and typically shows like "Leave it to Beaver" or some other family oriented show. Today, TV has gone wild and you can see just about anything going at any time of the day or night. There use to be a standard where certain shows were only viewed after 10 o'clock. Well, you can turn your television on right now and I guarantee you will see a commercial or a show talking about, showing, or supporting sex in some form or fashion. For example, there are several commercials on TV throughout the course of a day. The commercials are about how to help men gain an erection to last longer or how to enlarge a man's penis. I know this sounds pretty graphic, however this conversation is necessary because of where we are as a society. In America today, everything is based on feelings without principles when it should be based on principles rather than feelings. People are so concerned with how situations and circumstances make them feel. In today's society, a person's feelings or emotions are expressed in everything. I can freely state this because America was founded on biblical principles. Remember when prayer was in the school? One woman felt it needed to be taken out and what happened? Prayer was taken out of the school based on how one woman felt about prayer in the school. This story reveals how one's feelings and emotions for pleasure can make a terrible mixture for pain.

The Pain In Pleasure

I remember being in 1st grade and hanging out with my cousin during class, at recess, or in the cafeteria and we would try and touch girls inappropriately. Well, the two of us would get behind girls and feel on their derriere while waiting in line to go to the bathroom, cafeteria, etc. We would fake an accident or find some way to brush up against them just to touch them. We really didn't know the true depth of what we were really doing but that was the mindset that we had at the tender age of six. Think about this: these two innocent little boys devised a plan on gaining pleasure from feeling on little girls in their class. This may sound strange or weird to you or you may be laughing at the fact that you know someone who did this or maybe you did it at some time or another. Of course, at this point, no one had touched, fondled, or sexually abused either one of us. So how did we get to this point where we are thinking about sex and carrying out the acts of inappropriate touching? The bible teaches us that we are born in a world of sin and shapened in iniquity. Therefore our very nature can cause us to sin, not that this should be a reason to continue in sin. The bible also talks about the fact that each generation becomes more wicked than the previous generation. It is my sincere hope that if you are reading this book, and you have children, this information will cause you to do some early investigation and provide some possible intervention for your children. At least be open to having the conversation about sex or asking some questions.

It is interesting how my cousin and I would find pleasure in talking about the things that we would do or imagine the things we would do sexually to girls in our first grade class. Sounds sick, I know, but these are the things that some boys talk about, not really knowing the depth of what is being discussed or the seriousness of what they are engaging themselves in. I remember I would spend summers in the country with my grandpa who took care of my cousin who was also my best friend. We would lay in the bed late at night and, for what seemed like hours, we would tell stories about what we would do to girls we liked. Now these conversations were never that explicit, the bulk of what we talked about was touching them on the hind parts and kissing them, none of which either of us had

The Pain In Pleasure

really done at that point. So, as you can see, we were just two boys with great imaginations telling stories about what we would do. We compared our stories until we would fall asleep at night. As I write now, I think about the doors we were opening up in our lives. Here we are, in the first grade, speaking about things we really had no idea of and this was during a time the most you saw on TV was "Leave it to Beaver" where Ward and June Cleaver slept in separate beds. So, where did these thoughts come from and why were we speaking on them and gaining pleasure that we had not yet experienced? In fact, where did the idea come from?

This sounds kind of harmless, but I have learned about the power of words and speaking things into existence. I have also learned about strongholds and how we open up the door to our life for the enemy to send suggestions to us based on the things we allow to consume our time and imaginations. These suggestions come in the form of a commercial in our minds that motivates us to do things we know that we should not do. But because these are things we want to do, even though we know it's wrong (we seek to please our flesh), we do them anyway even if we don't have the power to fight against the enemy of our soul. Our soul is our greatest commodity and sometimes we sell it or give it away as if it has no value at all.

The bible teaches that words have power and we could speak life or death with our words. With that thought in mind, it helps me realize that my words have gotten me into some trouble. See, at a very early age I'm laying around confessing and speaking things that would later come back to cause me much grief. I don't know about girls but a lot of the boys I grew up with would sit around and talk about girls and the things that they have done or wanted to do to them. Ultimately, what we were doing was opening up doors to strongholds in our lives. I never really shared any of my dirt with others but whether I was doing it at these times or not, just being around that type of environment was dangerous because of what I exposed myself to. People can become a product of their environment.

The things boys often talk about aren't always productive. Some boys, and even girls, sit around and talk

The Pain In Pleasure

about each other in a very degrading way. For example, boys will often tell girls that what's between me and you is between me and you. Well, what girls fail to realize is that the first opportunity most boys get they are going to tell somebody, that person tells another and before you know it, everyone knows what was said and done. What happens at this point is that the pleasure you had just became painful and embarrassing for the individual who thought you would keep their secret.

In most cases, this can be extremely embarrassing to you and your family. It's nothing worse than for your mother or father to find out that you did something that they would not be pleased with you doing. A good parent will have some form of discipline that will cause the desire of that pleasure to be washed completely away.

Analogy: Proper Rules of Engagement

James 1:19-20, be quick to listen, slow to respond, and slow to wrath:

Growing up in the early 70's and 80's, I was taught that you can do anything you set your mind and heart to do. The number one key component to accomplishing my goals was attributed to getting a good, solid education. I would often hear the expression that a good education, along with a good attitude, will take you a long way in life. This simple but common statement was the driving force behind the average American home.

Parents today raise their children with a similar but very different slogan. They raise their children to believe that they can do anything. The concerns I have with statements are the valuable information often left out. The importance of not having to read between the lines to make decisions increases the chances of making better decisions in life. As people, we need everything in between in order to fully understand what and how to respond correctly. Then, and only then, can we make good, God-conscious decisions.

Key Principles Left Out

1. Love the Lord God with all of your heart and soul.
2. Love your neighbors as yourself and really mean it (keeping in mind your neighbor is everyone you come in

The Pain In Pleasure

contact with). Respect yourself, others and especially those in authority over you.

When we learn or teach this practice without proper rules of engagement or directions to follow, there is too much filling in the blanks __ __ __. Filling in the blanks without proper instructions and principles to follow can lead to failure. I can fill in the blanks with anything that sounds good to me—for instance, gaining too much responsibility at one time or making decisions based on what sounds good or right to you without seeking wise counsel.

When we are taught just to gain things without the understanding of why we should and how we should or should not, it has a reverse affect on our lives. Here we have three good examples of this statement, stated differently but with the same meaning, "What so ever a man sowed he shall also reap" "What goes around comes around" "When you dig one ditch you better dig two because the ditch you dig for me just might be for you." People often hear what they want to hear but if we at least attempt to teach proper bible principles in a very detailed and precise manner, we could decrease or even prevent a lot of heart ache and pain.

Simply put, it can prevent a whole lot of the pain in pleasure, because we now have the opportunity to learn how not to do whatever it takes to get what we want or gain access by any means necessary.

Lesson learned:

The rules of engagement were designed to build your relationship with God through his son Jesus Christ. Gaining a good education is fine, believing you can accomplish everything you set out to accomplish is great but nothing is successful without God being in the center. The bible says, Seek ye first the Kingdom of God. Seeking God first before we make decision prevents us from making the same mistakes over and over again.

Analogy: **First Love Blues**

If you have ever had the experience of having a first love and you truly believe it was true love how did it affect you? Here we have Steve remembering his first love. Steve and Cynthia are in love in the 8th grade and, of course by now, they have already started having sex outside of marriage. So here Steve is, in love at about 13

The Pain In Pleasure

years old; he believed that it was love because before these feelings had erupted, he had plenty of female friends or girlfriends. This time it appeared to be very different because they were spending countless hours on the phone, at her house, at basketball games, or wherever. They would literally fall asleep on the phone at night talking about nothing. This is how it all began—spending all of this unsupervised time together. They were both really good kids at home, school, and in the community. I guess that's why their parents permitted them to spend so much time alone together. This time alone started out as completely innocent until they both got a little too warm and kissing just wasn't enough anymore. The once innocent, late night conversations have now turned into something totally different. Steve and Cynthia began to talk about things you wouldn't even imagine that two young and innocent people would be talking about over the phone or at any time, like having phone sex.

So now they started planning on how they could make their heated conversations happen, you know, on those late night calls where she tells him she loves him and he tells her he loves her. In the course of the false love affair comes the statement, "If you love me you will do this for me (have sex)." The pressure is definitely increasing more and more from here. So now it's on! Here they are experimenting with sex at her house on the couch, or at Friendship Park on the ground. Things heated up so much that whenever they were alone, chances are they were either doing it or touching one another inappropriately. This began getting so out of control it became even more risky each time, because when you start to have sex it's like crack, you got to have it more and more.

Listen to this wild example. There was one occasion when they were at a basketball game and somehow either Steve convinced Cynthia, or she just did it, but she laid her head on his lap as if she was tired and in a crowd of people she performed ____ ___ you fill in the blanks on that one. Trust me, this isn't about promoting fornication, it's all about promoting awareness! Do you know what your children are doing when they are out with their friends? Do you even want to know what type of pain this pleasure could cause them or you?

The Pain In Pleasure

Of course, being all hot and bothered, they leave the game and go do what they do or what they had been doing. The young man's famous slogan was it didn't matter when, where, or how they did it as long as they did it together. This slogan has worked for years with both young, undisciplined girls to outright silly women who can be convinced to please or pleasure this particular individual. If you were to deal with him you had to adopt his philosophy. If only they knew that the wages of sin was death. They were sinning as much as they could. The pain in some pleasures we desire slowly kills us without us even knowing. The only things we think about are, as long as I don't get her pregnant or catch some disease then I'm good. What do we do? We say I'm not hurting anyone and I'm the only one being affected by what I'm doing.

So here they are, they leave the basketball game at the high school and go outside on the far end of the band hall to do what they do with no shame in what they were doing or where they were doing it.

Pleasure is great when you don't know what you are doing is ultimately opening up doors that you have no control over. The two of them were dying in the process of having what you would call fun or meeting your physical needs. Here they are on the ground, in the back of the school, by the band hall thinking they have found a great spot to get it on, regardless of the wet ground or the outdoors. The only goal they have in mind is to please themselves and to do it now. Besides, they aren't hurting anyone. Everything is going great and they are in the middle of doing "the do" and out of nowhere shows up Cynthia's girl friend, the one she rode to the game with and catches them in the act of having sex. Just minutes ago, they thought they discovered a great spot where no one could possibly find them. Wow, pleasure just became physical pain. Why? Because they got caught doing what they had been doing alone in secret. The pain they experienced at that very moment was just the surface pain of getting caught and feeling some embarrassment. They didn't even realize the spiritual pain of unlocking and feeding the lust demon that lay deep down inside of them.

They immediately got their clothing back on and rushed back to the gym feeling extremely embarrassed. The

The Pain In Pleasure

girl immediately runs and tells her mother, which was a great choice. This was a good choice the friend made. They were extremely upset because they didn't want to be exposed for the things they were already doing. Immediately the young lady's mom takes them both and leaves the game angry. I'm sure in the back of the lady's mind she is thinking, "Here I am taking them to the game and this girl is outside on the ground having sex under my watch." As a parent writing this, I would be furious if this happened with my daughter or someone's daughter I had under my care.

The young man is walking home from the game trying to figure out how he is going to come up with a lie good enough to tell his mother to get out of this world of trouble he's facing once he gets home. He got home and his mom hadn't found out yet, so he decided he would just tell her the truth of the matter and see where it goes because of the inner conviction. Steve wasn't accustomed to lying and especially not to his mother.

So, he's in the middle of sharing with his mother his version of the story; of course, now they are exposed.

Exposing the truth is the start of relinquishing pride and embarrassment over sins that we don't want our parents or people we love to know about us. We, as people of a sinful nature, are encouraged by satan and his demonic forces to hide our personal sins from our parents and spiritual leaders. This is especially true when they don't know what we have done or have been doing without them finding out!

Lesson learned:

Children often believe that the life they live has never been lived before. The bible teaches that there is nothing new under the sun. Kids have to learn to wholeheartedly listen to the parents who are teaching them about this subject matter. Parents must take time to talk to their children and share the importance of sex and abstinence.

The Bible teaches us to confess our sins one to another, but our pride convinces us that people are only out to harshly judge us and that prevents us from doing so. This form of pride will cause or lead us into destruction every time we choose to hide or cover up those things that our evil imagination convinces us to do.

The Pain In Pleasure

1 John 1:9 (New International Version)

"If we confess our sins, he is faithful and just and will forgive us our sins and purify us from all unrighteousness."

Proverbs 6:25 (New International Version)

"Do not lust in your heart after her beauty or let her captivate you with her eyes."

~~~~~~~~~~

Analogy: Early Exposure to Sex

Let's talk about sex! Well, sex for me has been a part of my life since I was about six years old! Yes, I said six years old. Sigmund Fraud states that a child starts to masturbate at around 3 years of age, based on his research. The research, of course, shares that the masturbation isn't sexual in nature but the act of pleasure is involved with the touching. For example, you may find your male child with his hands in his pants touching or feeling on himself, or your female child who gyrates or humps on your legs. What you have is the body being stimulated by pleasure, however the mind hasn't been exposed to the sexual nature or knowledge as to what to do. In my observation of children, I have noticed this to be true. I base this on the observation of boys and girls humping on the ground furniture or people. This, to me, supports Freud's theory of masturbation as early as three years of age.

So you take that theory and add what boys talk about and what do you have? You have a willing vessel. I was a willing ignorant vessel. Of course, I will never disclose who this person was that was only a few years older than me, but here was a 6 year old and a 10 year old having sex, or the act of physically pleasuring themselves, based on what they perceived to be intercourse. I think the term for this is considered "dry humping" in the world today. However, can you imagine the places your evil mind can really take you, especially the mind of innocent children?

Wow, look at that, having sex at 6 and 10 during the mid to late 70's based on boys talking and a girl who at 9 or 10 initiated it. There you have me, a willing vessel. Of course you're shocked and appalled, but what about you

The Pain In Pleasure

and your children? Do you know if they are having sex or not? Furthermore, have you taken the time to actually sit down and talk to them about the subject of sex? If you haven't, please stop reading now and go do it. As you can see, this book is all about ungodly pleasures.

So now you have a boy who knows nothing about sex but he has been talking about sex with his best friend, and they stay up late at night swapping stories about what they want to do to the girls they like in their first grade class. The boys even devised a plan as to how to get some pleasure out of feeling on the girls' bottoms.

Has this story started causing you any pain yet, realizing that a young boy is seeking pleasure and has now discovered it? I hope so! I pray that you will be provoked to talk to your sons and daughters about this important topic, before some predator or person that doesn't know very much will.

The problem we experience when it comes to talking about sex with our children is that we are too embarrassed to have the conversation with them. You can easily get over this embarrassment, but your son or daughter contracting a life threatening disease, or having a baby out of wedlock will alter their entire lives. You tell me which one would you rather have: the embarrassment or life altering experience?

Talking about sex is a very important topic that parents should be thrilled to talk to their children about! Children shouldn't feel embarrassed talking to their parents about sex. This responsibility falls on the parent to discover a creative way of making this conversation easy for everyone. This conversation should take place very early in life with children and parents. I would say as early as five or six years of age. I believe the conversations should start there and continue as the mind of the child and parent grows. Wisdom should be applied to this matter and age appropriate language should be used. I recommended the age six based on the fact that at around first grade or second grade, boys and girls begin to identify classmates that they admire. Some will already have given a title to a boy or girl they like as their boyfriend or girlfriend. The average person is in the first grade by six years of age and second grade by seven or

The Pain In Pleasure

even eight years, so if you wait too long after six years of age, the child has already been involved in several relationships that you may or may not be aware of. Some parents think it's so cute for their little six year old to have a girlfriend or boyfriend. Wake up parents! That's not all Satan or evil imagination. This is a loving parent providing help for future failure in the life of their children. Now that's pain in pleasure. So, I suggest you began talking to your children at about six years of age. I know many people will disagree with my philosophy but, again, I'm sharing from my personal experience as a child and my experience as a father and educator.

Talking about sex can be a bit awkward for both the parent and the child. However, the conversation could prevent children from making adult decisions during their school-aged years. God's word says, our people perish because of the lack of knowledge. This knowledge is often possessed by a parent who refuses to talk about sex because it's too embarrassing or they feel that the school or someone other than them should be responsible for teaching their kids about sex. Pleasure will leave behind pain that you would never be able to explain or imagine. "Boys Before Books Brings Babies." Boys don't bring babies home to stay, maybe a short visit at best. They don't experience the sleepless nights with a teething, feverish or hungry baby. Those pains are experienced mostly by the grandmother and the baby's mother. The pain in pleasure is so unforgettable. Please view these important scriptures that every parent and parent-to-be should know.

Proverbs 22:6 (Amplified Bible)
"Train up a child in the way he should go [and in keeping with his individual gift or bent], and when he is old he will not depart from it."

Ephesians 6:4 (Amplified Bible)
"Fathers, do not irritate and provoke your children to anger [do not exasperate them to resentment], but rear them [tenderly] in the training and discipline and the counsel and admonition of the Lord."

2 Timothy 3:15 (Amplified Bible)
"And how from your childhood you have had a knowledge of and been acquainted with the sacred

The Pain In Pleasure

Writings, which are able to instruct you and give you the understanding for salvation which comes through faith in Christ Jesus [through the leaning of the entire human personality on God in Christ Jesus in absolute trust and confidence in His power, wisdom, and goodness]."

CHAPTER 4

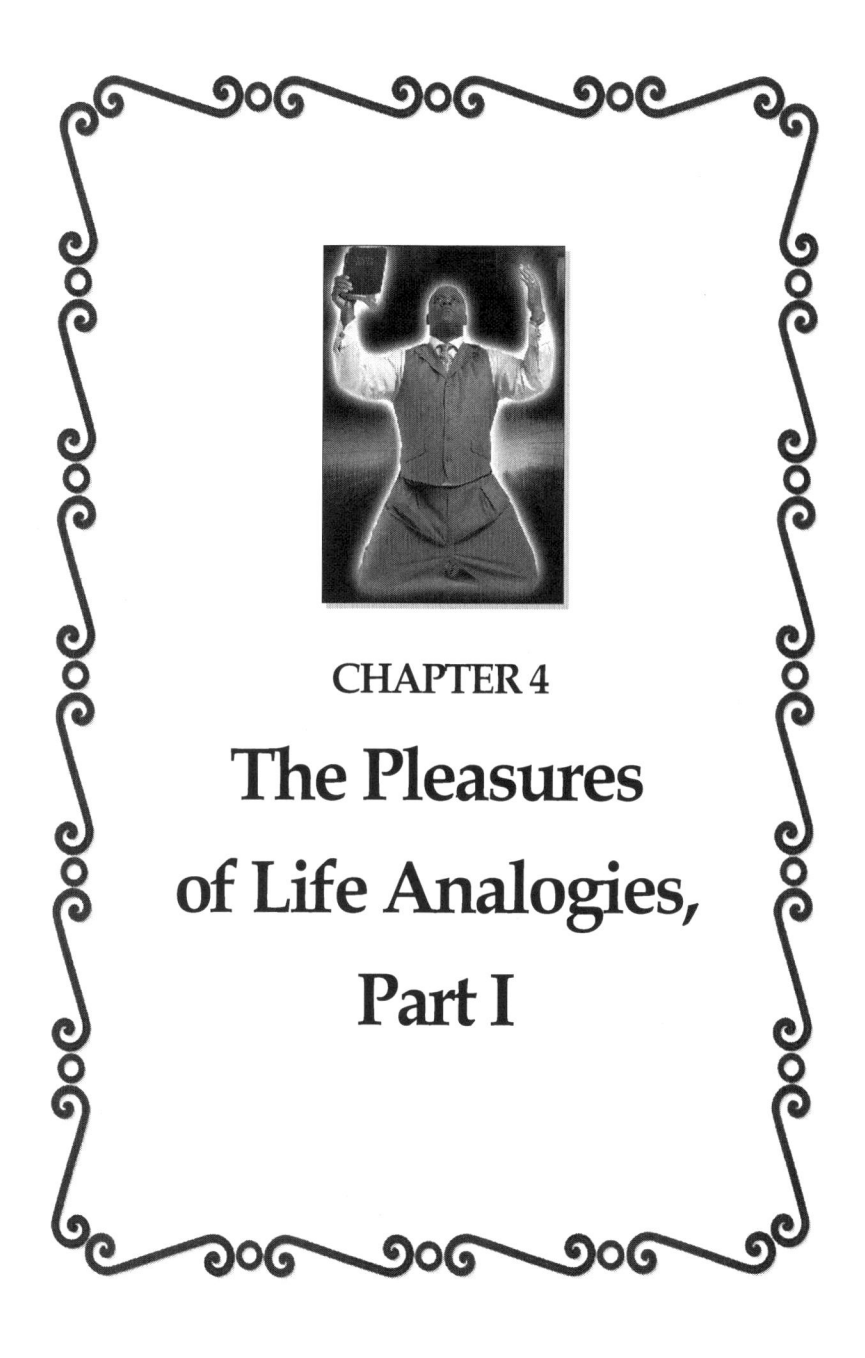

The Pleasures of Life Analogies, Part I

The Pleasures of Life Analogies, Part I

Analogy: Who Is the Baby's Daddy?

Mr. Barry Andrew Jackson your name has been submitted as the birth father of Michelle Nicole Hood, born December 1, 1990 to Ms. Sheila Alexander Hood of Atlanta, Georgia. Mr. Jackson, your name was listed as one of the potential candidates as the father of the above listed child. You are hereby ordered by the courts of Georgia to appear for DNA testing for the above listed child.

"What?!" I live in Maryland. I'm not leaving my good job to go take some crazy DNA test. In fact, I can't leave my job to go to Atlanta to take some stupid DNA test. I don't even have that kind of time or money to do it! Lord, this has got to be a sick joke. I know I am not this baby's daddy. Who is Michelle Hood anyway? Lord, I don't even remember a female named Michelle. Who in the world is Michelle and why is she putting my name in her baby drama? This woman has got to be some kind of trickster looking to get some money out of me.

Okay, let me re-read this letter. I know these people got to be making a mistake by sending me some certified letter to my job over some girl I slept with in high school years ago. How in the world did they locate me?

Mr. Barry Andrew Jackson, your name has been submitted as the birth father of Michelle Nicole Hood, born December 1, 1990 to Ms. Sheila Alexander Hood of Atlanta, Georgia. Mr. Jackson your name was listed as one of the potential candidates as the father of the above listed child. You are hereby ordered by the courts of Georgia to appear for DNA testing for the above listed child.

Are you kidding me? This happened over ten years ago. How am I supposed to remember that far back? When I was in high school, I slept with plenty of females. I am not aware of any pregnancy issues from any of them. This has got to be a huge mistake. I was in high school having fun and Lord you know I can't even remember sleeping with this individual. Please God, this can't be happening to me.

Let me calm down and try to think of all the females I slept with back in high school. Lord Jesus, please

The Pain In Pleasure

don't let this be true. God, I'll do anything if you just get me out of this situation, besides, Lord, I don't even know this woman.

Now that I think of it, Lord I thank you because I remember this girl now! Everyone called her by her nickname but she claimed that someone else was this baby's daddy. But, now she is putting me in the middle of this mess. I know for sure I never slept with this girl unprotected. Man, I had to be a stone fool for sleeping with this girl in the first place. She was just a jump-off in high school and everybody was tapping that back in the day.

This woman must really be crazy! She knows good and well that her baby isn't mine. How dare she bring me into this drama and ruin my life.

Michelle knows she was screwing around with a ton of brothers besides me. That baby can be from any number of other brothers. Lord, what am I going to do?

Oh God, let me think. Could I have slipped once and slept with this girl unprotected? Could the condom have broken and I didn't notice it? Man, what am I thinking about? I never slept with this girl without a condom and I know for a fact no condom ever broke on me. Okay, let me calm down. I'm just going to take this test and pray with all my heart that this baby is not mine.

Lesson Learned

High school is a period when many young people don't use wisdom or common sense. During this stage of life, most students or individuals don't think past the here and now. Therefore, they don't see the long term affect their decisions may have. They do not realize that a moment of pleasure can have a lasting effect.

The analogy you just read shows how decisions we make can affect us. No matter how long ago it was, decisions can come back and haunt us. The baby is the only real victim in this case; certainly not Mr. Jackson nor the baby's mother.

They both decided to make adult decisions with their bodies which could have resulted in any number of repercussions.

This type of thinking doesn't necessarily have anything to do with socio-economic statues, nor ethnic background. Any person, regardless of age, has to be

The Pain In Pleasure

completely insane to sleep around, period. However, it is ten times worse when we sleep with people we care nothing about. The young man was cool, laying down and getting back up, but the possibilities of being a father to a child, he wanted nothing to do with that. Premarital sex is extremely dangerous and should be compared to smoking crack or something along those lines. It appears to be fun while it lasts but now the individual's life is hanging in the valley of some DNA test. My hope would be that hindsight really is 20/20 for this individual and that his thinking will be different if faced with this situation again.

If I only knew then what I know now surely I wouldn't have made such quick decisions based on what made me feel good. This is a statement most wise adults would or could attest too now that age and wisdom has, hopefully, kicked in.

The Bible teaches us to abstain from fornication (sex) until after marriage. This principle seems to be extremely challenging once you have already tasted the forbidden fruit. I believe that is why God said wait until you are married before engaging in sex. Sex before marriage exposes one to an appetite of unbridled, lustful desires.

This biblical principle, if followed, could have prevented any possibilities of receiving this letter or case. The person's response to receiving the letter is rather common in most cases, but had he not been involved with having premarital sex, he would have been 100 percent sure. In high school or even now, most people deal strictly with the here and now and what makes them feel good, giving little or no thought to the consequences of their actions. The amazing thing is the response to the letter caused the person to instantly call on the Lord. This is a natural response to a person in trouble. My only concern with this particular kind of response to God is the relationship or lack of relationship that the individual currently has when making the statement. Please don't misunderstand me, any time you need help, you should call on Jesus Christ and He will respond. Does the conversation and communication end once the problem is resolved? The genuine concern here is about building an effective relationship with God. This type of response comes from people who may or may not have a true relationship with God. Give thought to this question: How

The Pain In Pleasure

would you feel if a person only calls on you when they're in trouble? How would you respond to them?

I take this time to stop and pray, "Lord please forgive all of the foolish mistakes made by students in high school. I pray that every high school, middle school and elementary student throughout the world would realize that pleasure can bring you pain and that they realize everything that looks good and sounds good isn't always good for you. I pray that every ungodly open door be closed. In Jesus' name, Amen."

This prayer is made simply because most people have some basic knowledge of how God feels about pre-marital sex/fornication but they choose not to follow it. The question I wish I had the answer to is what causes us to purposefully not follow God's commandments? For example, this next scripture is a wonderful example of how our selfish will and our fleshly desires convince us to go against God's plan for our life.

"When the woman saw that the fruit of the tree was good for food and pleasing to the eye, and also desirable for gaining wisdom, she took some and ate it. She also gave

some to her husband, who was with her, and he ate" (Genesis 3:6).

This very popular scripture has been viewed and disputed in various ways and for many reasons. Please go with me as I attempt to analyze this text for the relationship and meaning surrounding the very creation of "The Pain in Pleasure." The subject is rotated around the word "obey." Obey God's commands and His principles for a victorious Christian life.

If we obey God's word, He will work out His purpose and His true plan for our lives. The scripture you just read in Genesis is a snapshot of the life of Adam and Eve. The scripture gives insight to the mind and the deception it sometimes gives us. The command God gave to Adam and Eve was they could eat from every tree in the garden except from the tree of the knowledge of good and evil. The fruit was pleasing to the eye and tasted good to eat, she gave to Adam, her husband, and he ate it also. The lust of the eyes causes men and women to see one another in ways that they shouldn't. Because they like what they see, they often seek to have what they want

The Pain In Pleasure

without giving much regard to whom it may or may not affect. Does this mean we should not be attracted to people or to not look at people? No, this simply means that with the principles that God has put in place, we must discipline ourselves to obey His word. We are not to act on things that stimulate us simply because we can or because it looks good to us. People can become so attracted to one another that they feel they have to have each other physically. The young man in the analogy obviously slept with women just because he could. Perhaps, the young lady he slept with was pleasing to his eyes as was the fruit to Adam and Eve. How often have you made decisions or acted against God's word all because you liked what you saw? That's the pain in pleasure I'm hoping to expose every born again believer to.

One can become extremely disheartened through the realization that a lifetime of good can be forever blemished by a single sin or a poor decision. The consequences can be seemingly immeasurable to the mind of the individual most affected by the decision he or she has made. In the case of Adam and Eve, the consequences of their sin affected the entire world for the rest of time. When Adam and Eve ate the fruit, they never imagined all the harm that their one sin would cause. A good example of that can be explained through the basic terminology and understanding of generational curses that some pleasures of life often birth. The scripture that tells us "obedience is better than sacrifice" is a fair warning to us all.

Often, we as parents never think that our sins will and can be passed on to our children. If we choose not to gain deliverance and provide a watchful eye over our children, that is exactly what will happen. Sin doesn't present itself as hurtful or dangerous. Rather, it presents itself in various ways, such as through deception or selfishness. It is the act of doing what I want to do, even if it is an ungodly act, no matter to whom it may affect, as long as I'm pleased. Human nature is sinful and in my sinful nature I seek to sin in my flesh, mind, or any other area I seek to discover ungodly pleasures. I believe that we often forget that there is a war going on and we are in the middle of that war. The enemy of your soul is not taking prisoners, he's destroying lives and, more importantly, souls. We must

The Pain In Pleasure

be aware that the greatest commodity any individual possesses is his soul.

So you're probably thinking this writer is a bit extreme or some type of religious freak! On average, most people don't really give thought to all of the so called little sins that we commit daily without repentance. The bible teaches or instructs Christians to renew their minds daily, but I would go even further by saying that sometimes it's necessary to renew our minds several times throughout the day. I say this because we take so many things, throughout the course of an average day, into our system or spirit that contaminates us.

Think about this, if you truly evaluate your day, you would discover that there are several things that you did or didn't do correctly... things you did not handle correctly according to biblical principles designed by God.

~~~~~~~~~~

Analogy: **The Simple Lie**

For example: Someone walks up and asks, "How's your day going?" and you immediately lie to them by saying it's going fine or it's going great. In your heart you know that you are one more question away from losing your patience, your head is pounding from a headache, or maybe you're worried about your children. The bizarre thing about this kind of response is that most people will think or even feel that this response is perfectly fine. The fact of the matter is that you told a lie. You didn't want anyone to know what was really going on in your world. You don't have to tell people all of your personal business but you could have simply said, "Today isn't the best day but I'm trusting in the Lord for a positive change." People often tell lies without any real thought to it at all, unless someone brings it to their attention. This happens simply because it is easy to cover up the truth from people and, chances are, unless I share the truth with you, you will never know the truth about my day. The true nature of sin is most often covered by selfish pleasures or desires. People tell simple lies when they know all along, deep down within their heart, that the answer they gave was simply not the truth. These lies are told daily by people who answer questions based on their emotional highs and lows. These actions are most often noted based on the

The Pain In Pleasure

Holy Scriptures that teach us to cast down all evil imaginations. The evil imagination doesn't appear to harm anyone initially, but scriptures teach us that as a man thinks in his heart, so is he. Simply put, if you think or imagine something long enough, you will discover a way of putting it into action.

Research shows that men, in particular, think about sex a very large percentage of their day in various ways. A person who thinks about sex all the time will soon begin to masturbate and or become addictive to pornography. This still seems pretty harmless to some, especially to the one that's involved with the acts. Masturbation appears to only affect the individual who is masturbating but sooner or later he or she is going to crave something more than just pictures and imagination. The result could be rape, incest, child molestation, or any number of things that could cause harm to one's self or to others. These small acts have deep-rooted, spiritual affects that most individuals, caught up in them, never give thought to.

This is a clear demonstration of one's pleasure taking control and now pain has been inflicted at the detriment of another's suffering. Sexual crimes normally begin with a thought or the imagination that has spiraled out of control. The principle of casting down all evil imagination could have prevented a lot of people from being incarcerated.

Let's face it, sin disguises itself and initially looks pleasing and harmless, but the final result is always death. I believe that if we, the chosen people of God, receive Christ Jesus in our lives and truly understand the impact of sin and the controlling power it has over our lives, we will choose not to sin. For the wages of sin is death, but the gift of God is eternal life. I believe if we would just trust God, we would choose to live and not die. I further believe that to truly relate to the very essence of this statement, we must understand the spiritual concept behind its true meaning.

The bible teaches us that some men's sins go before him and some men's sins follow after him. In the case of the young man in the analogy of the DNA test, he would never have been in that position had he not disobeyed God's principles on fornication.

The Pain In Pleasure

One way of viewing this scripture in simplicity, or to obtain a clearer understanding, would be to view it from a natural sense.

When viewing or researching scriptures, they are often better understood when compared to a natural situation. The example I am choosing to use to explain this scripture is surrounded by the premises that some parents choose to give out consequences immediately and some will extend grace for a later date. I believe to further illustrate this scripture is to share that some deaths come immediately and some deaths come slowly. Some people are killed immediately in the acts of their sin and some slowly die such as in the cases of HIV and AIDS.

Analogy: David & Melissa

Hello David, how in the world are you doing? Wow, it has really been a long time since we last spoke. In fact, it has been way too long. How are the wife and the children doing? Everyone is doing wonderfully Melissa. I agree, girl it has been way too long, and how is that husband of yours treating you? How is your family doing? Great, the kids are growing so fast and my husband really loves me and gives me just about everything I want. Wow, that's great. You must be the happiest Woman in the world. Well, I don't know about all that, but I'm happy! If the brother is giving you everything you want, then what in the world could possibly be the problem? I mean you are happy aren't you? Well Melissa, aren't you? You know you can talk to me; we go back like car seats girl. Well, he makes me happy in certain areas if you know what mean! Certain areas? Certain areas like what? Well, I don't really want to talk about it David because it's kind of embarrassing to me! Melissa girl you know you can talk about anything with me. Alright David, you are right since I know you and trust you, what harm can it be? Maybe you can help by given me a man's perspective. Okay then, spill the beans. What's the brother's problem? I know you're a wonderful woman so something has got to be wrong with him. David, when I tell you all but one area, I'm sure you know exactly what a woman is talking about. I mean don't forget you know me. You know what I like and you knew just what to do to get me there. Melissa, I know you

The Pain In Pleasure

have got to be kidding me, because I know it's not sex, or is it? Yes, David, I can't even front or believe it myself, but his sex drive is just not like mine. Besides that, there are certain things he doesn't like doing. He claims it's because of the baby but to me, it's all crazy. When he finally does it, I'm just not pleased. Melissa Baby, have you tried to communicate with the brother about what you like and what you need? Yes, I have even written him letters and everything, but the brother just isn't getting it. What's his excuse or response when you share how you feel about what's going on with his behavior toward your needs? He claims he's tired because he works long hours and David that is true but still that is no excuse for leaving me undone. I tell him I work long hours cooking for the whole family, clean the entire house and taking care of everything concerning the kids. Wow Melissa, that's strange, crazy even, what man doesn't want to have sex on a regular? I don't care how long he has worked. Hmmm, so tell me more about this situation with your man. Wow, Melissa I'm so sorry to hear about this. I can really relate to this situation one hundred percent. I thought it was just because women didn't enjoy sex as much or it just wasn't thought about by women as much as men. No David that is not the case. Wow, my wife is the same way. I love her, but she just doesn't seem to get it, want it, or need it as much as I do. Melissa she actually makes me feel like there is something wrong with me. Have you tried to share with him just how you feel? Yes, I most certainly have and on some occasions he does well for a day or two and then it's back to the same old routine? I understand that he works long hours but a sister still has needs. Amen to that! I don't feel like I should have to constantly tell my husband over and over again what I need. David I'm so frustrated I don't have a clue as to what to do? The man simply just doesn't get it.

    The two married people decide to hook up after months of sharing their individual frustration with their marriage. One thing leads to another and the two end up in bed, sleeping with one another because their spouses don't satisfy them the way they think they should. Therefore, they feel justified in sleeping with one another. The two of them feel that they connect on physical levels

The Pain In Pleasure

that their spouses can't or won't attempt to. The two of them provided the sexual peak or climax of sexual pleasure for each other, unlike his wife or her husband had done before or they even imagined. The relationship gives them the opportunity to be sexually happy if only for brief moments and opportunities. The only thing that they rely on is that when they do get together, their physical frustration is temporarily over.

Lesson learned:

In some cases, temporary moments of pleasure can have potential destruction for life. This destruction has a lasting effect on everyone who loves you. The bible teaches that men should love their wives as Christ loves the church and gave Himself for it. Anyone who knows the church, understands that the people are often very difficult and challenging to love. Loving the church means putting up with and dealing with things that the natural mind couldn't began to imagine or think of. Marriage is a very challenging task, however it is not impossible. There are many people who have been successfully married for 48 years or more. In those 48 years, I'm sure there have been good, bad, and even crazy moments suffered by both individuals. However, love had to conquer it all.

This kind of love covers a multitude of sin. An analogy such as this example with Melissa and David is not an excuse to cheat but an opportunity to address important marital concerns and move forward. This love also expresses that no matter what happens in marriage, you endure the good, the bad and the ugly, based on your guidance of the Holy Spirit and wise counsel. Wise counsel is a must because, often times, it is essential to have a voice of reason to bring to light to the importance of allowing God, through the Holy Spirit, to manage and control the marriage.

The two people in this particular example confided mostly with their inner-personal desires rather than with their marriage partners. This could have been a wonderful opportunity to seek marriage counseling for the marriages. Perhaps counseling could have helped or insisted that all parties involved be reminded of the moral and ethical vows and commitment that they made to one another in

The Pain In Pleasure

front of their friends, families, loved ones, and most of all, God. Should David and Melissa alone be blamed for their actions? How much responsibility should their spouses take for not responding to their needs?

Some single people would ask, "Why do married people get married if they're going to cheat?" This can only be described as selfishness at its highest degree because they only thought about their own desires when they decided to hook up and cheat on their partners. One would ask, "Do they really love their mate?" I would venture to say, "Yes," but they love themselves more, both the cheaters as well as the neglectors.

When making decisions in life, it is a wonderful practice to think about the people who love us. What if they found out or somehow discovered just what you have done? How would they feel about your actions and what cause or affect would it have on them? Divorce rates are at an all time high and children are the ones most affected by the selfish decisions of the parents. God highly honors marriage, which He instituted at creation.

Let's analyze several ways this source of pleasure turns into pain.

A. The husband or wife catches them in the act of having sex and kills them. Crimes of passion happen every single day across the world and now the other partner is incarcerated for 25 years to life.

B. The two never get caught but as a result, a baby is born. The spouse finds out and their moments of pleasure could possibly cause the family a lifetime of disappointment and pain.

C. They didn't get caught, no baby is born, but what he didn't know is that she has been carrying a deadly virus for years and discovers that he is HIV positive from a routine physical.

D. The guilt from being unfaithful haunts the marriage daily not allowing the individual total freedom to love and be loved by their partner.

These are just some examples of how pleasure can quickly become painful and last a lifetime.

The very essence of "The Pain in Pleasure" is the spiritual battle that's taking place with analogies just like this one. No one ever talks about this type of stuff. The church hasn't addressed these matters with the consistency or intensity that is needed for today's society. When people hear about examples like this one, their response is, "Oh what a shame" or "How could he?" or "She is just a whore." People often give lightness to the natural occurrence of things, but never consider the spiritual aspects of things. The reality of it all is pleasure has a great deal of pain attached to it especially when it goes against the principles of God.

~~~~~~~~~~~

Analogy: My Story, Your Story, and the God's Honest Truth

This analogy involves two people who have been intimately seeing one another for years. The relationship appears to work well for both of them and they appear to be happy with the relationship as it stands. The two of them haven't always been faithful to one another but they really believe that they have genuine love for one another. The relationship happens to click for both of them on every level and they both believe that there is a possibility for a brighter future together, although they don't often discuss the future. All of a sudden, out of the blue, the female decides that she no longer wants to take her birth control pills. She really doesn't share her reasons in great detail with the man she is currently dealing with.

The two of them discuss her decision to stop taking her birth control pills, however, the two of them aren't in agreement with the decision. They continue to have sexual relations as normal. This continues and nothing manifests, so all is well. Some time has passed and no discussion has come up about the subject of not taking the pills. The two of them freely continue to do what they do. Eventually, the young lady ends up pregnant and now the great relationship has turned into turmoil to the degree of termination.

They constantly argue over what they should do about this urgent matter. They are both older adults with career aspirations but now they aren't sure if their future together is as bright as it once looked. They both professed Christianity, but now their true moral values are on the line. The young lady has more of a desire to keep the child because she sees the possibilities of a future marriage and a

The Pain In Pleasure

family. The young man, in his mind, is completely against having another child out of wedlock. He has no insight on marriage or family at this time. Situations such as these can almost never come to a happy medium.

    The two of them disagree on whether they should keep the baby or not. They find themselves in an abortion clinic waiting to speak to a counselor minutes before the abortion is to actually take place. The counselor finally comes in and explains to them both the actual stage of the pregnancy and the progress of the fetus. The young lady finally comes to her senses and decides she doesn't want to go through with the abortion. The young man doesn't verbally agree or disagree, but cowardly expresses that it is ultimately her decision. They abruptly leave the clinic together. During the ride home, there's no conversation, in fact, it is completely silent the entire trip. The two of them, quietly within themselves, decide not to call or speak to one another. Three weeks go by and the two have lost daily contact as normal, and, as a result, they have not spoken or seen each other. The situation becomes extremely awkward for them both.

The young lady's name is Kat and the young man's name is Lance. In the meantime, the young lady has moved to a nearby area. They both go on with their lives as normal. Three weeks after that long silent morning drive home from the abortion clinic, Kat gets a call from Lance.

"Hello Kat. How have you been doing? I just wanted let you know that I have been thinking long and hard about the decision with the baby. I know that I haven't really been there the way I should have since we left the clinic. I have finally come to my senses. I now know that my feelings were selfish and uncharacteristic of who I am and the principles I believe in. Kat, I have decided that I want us to keep the baby! I believe somehow things will work out in the end."

Kat breaks down and cries and asks Lance, "Are you for real?" Lance says, "Yes, I believe everything will work out!" Kat sadly informs him that she went ahead and had the abortion two weeks earlier. Lance is completely shocked and in disbelief about what Kat has done, based on the decision that was made at the clinic that day. They both began to cry over the decision Kat made, which ultimately

The Pain In Pleasure

affected both of their lives. Lance asked her why she would go forward after leaving the clinic the way she did. Kat shared with him that she decided that she did not want to bring another baby in the world under their current circumstance, and she believed that based on his response, it wasn't necessary to inform him. They both continued to cry hysterically realizing that they made a great mistake.

Lesson learned:

The lesson learned is that some pleasures can really become pain that lasts a lifetime and sometimes you have no control over another person's actions. Don't allow lust to drive you down the road to destruction. Kat and Lance are both presently married to other people and have moved on with their lives; but the pain of this one decision continues to haunt them. Did Lance take too long to reach out to Kat or did Kat act too quickly before taking one last opportunity to consult with Lance before taking matters into her own hands? Lance has his side of the story, Kat has her side of the story, but only God knows the truth of the matter. Pro-life would have prevented the tears and the disappointments of what could have, what should have, and what is. What Would Jesus Do?

~ ~ ~ ~ ~ ~ ~ ~ ~ ~

Analogy: Your Pleasure, Their Pain

Mitchell and Jasmine have been married for six months and have decided that the marriage isn't what they signed up for and as a result have separated. The marriage was not successful, however they managed to have two kids in between their times separated. Years have passed and the children have grown up and now Mitchell wants to get a divorce in order to re-marry. The two children have no idea what's going on with either mom or dad, and they are caught up in the middle of loving both mom and dad with all of their heart. In the children's mind, they somehow believe that mom and dad will eventually work things out and they will be one big happy family. The children are confused because they often see mom and dad display levels of intimate physical affection towards one another (sleeping together).

The final hours have come and now dad needs to explain to the children what's about to take place. Mitchell

The Pain In Pleasure

is terrified to share his new and exciting news with the children because his pleasures will totally interrupt their lives as they now know it. Mitchell doesn't have the heart or the courage it takes to share the information with them. Mitchell's problem is that he now realizes, for the first time, that in order for him to be happy he has to finally tell the truth about the lies he has been telling his children and their mother for years. Mitchell realized the pain that he is about to cause them. However, if he doesn't tell them he won't be able to obtain the pleasure he ultimately seeks with the new mate he has selected.

Mitchell seeks the help of his friend, Brock, for support in what to do in this life-changing situation. He chooses Brock for several reasons... one is because he's cowardly and doesn't want to deal with the real pain of it all.

Brock expresses to him that the children really need to know the truth from him and fast. Mitchell asks Brock if he would talk to them for him because he knew he didn't have the strength, courage or know how to do this difficult task. Brock agrees to talk to the children only with him being present, along with Brock's daughter, for support. The information is shared and the oldest child who clearly understands what is about to happen. She breaks down and cries uncontrollably while the younger child sits there, looking confused.

Lesson learned

The lesson is to always tell the truth and not lie to cover up your personal dirt that will some day be revealed. The biblical principle is that the truth will make you free. Children really do deserve to know the truth as soon as their at the age where they can clearly understand what's being said. Often adults use the excuse of not wanting to cause their loved one's or children to hurt or suffer by exposing them to the truth. The truth does hurt but the sooner you deal with the pain of knowing the truth, the sooner you can grow and heal from those scares. Mitchell not only refused to share the truth with the children, but he lived a lie in front of the children. This lie has caused the children to have false hope that one day mom and dad will eventually get back together. The game he ran not only hurt the children's mother but the children

The Pain In Pleasure

as well. The only person who seemed to come out the winner in this situation was Mitchell, but eventually the consequences of his actions will catch up with him.

~~~~~~~~~~

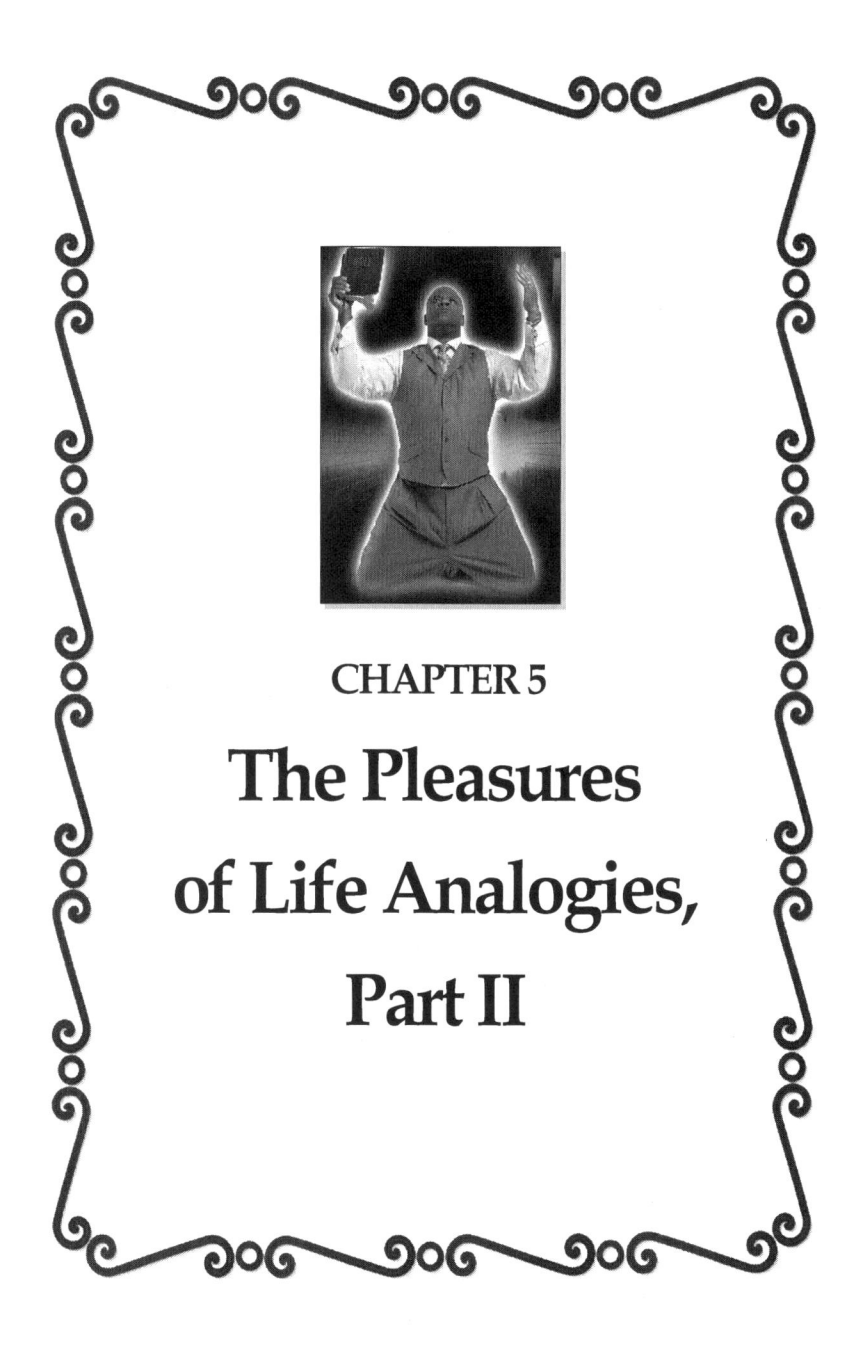

CHAPTER 5
The Pleasures of Life Analogies, Part II

The Pleasures of Analogies, Part II

Analogy: **Playing the Game**

Playing the game, can be fun until you realize it's a game you can't win. In life we can enter into games that we believe we can win or overcome until we realize we are in over our heads.

The game could start at different times for some people. Most often it begins in high school when a boy or girl decides that they will have two or more relationships with different people on the same level. This can happen intentionally or unintentionally but your response to it is what matters the most. I remember being popular in high school due to playing football and my physique, among other things, which made the girls aggressively attracted to me. Often times, I would see people take on a meaningless relationship; not because they were interested in the person, but because the person was interested in them. Let the games begin.

Analogy: **Best Friends, One Girl**

Two young men happen to be the best of friends;

one young man has a girlfriend and the other one doesn't. The three of them are all high school students and friends as well. The couple isn't that serious so all three talk on the phone separately and about different subjects on various occasions. All is going well with this until the couple begins to have problems for some reason or another. One day, the best friend and the girlfriend start talking on the phone and the girlfriend starts admiring the friend. The conversations begin to shift and spill over into an inappropriate conversation for the two of them to be having. Well, no one stops this behavior from happening and the friend doesn't know what's happening. Before you know it, the best friend is going over the girlfriend's house. One thing leads to another and the heat is on. This happens to be a turning point in the lives of the two friends, once the friend finds out what has happened. Now the pleasure that was once shared in the friendship becomes hurt and pain for all parties involved. Game over.

Analogy: Two Women, One Man

A young man decides that he is somewhat tired of dealing with a lot of different women so he narrows them

The Pain In Pleasure

down to two. The two women of course don't really know that they are competing until one day the young man decides that the day he normally gives to lady #1, he will give it to lady #2. Everything is working out well and the couple is off to a nice evening at the Frankie Beverly concert. The concert is nice and the evening is going extremely well until girl #1 discovers that the man she thought was hers and hers alone is out having a wonderful time at the Frankie Beverley concert with another woman. The whole time she thinks he's hard at work. How does she find out? She finds out through the hotline of one her best friends who decides she want to expose the rascal for who he really is, because she sees him at the concert with the other women. So girl #1 knows before the concert is over that this man she loves is being unfaithful and he is doing it at that very moment. What was meant to be a night of fun and pleasure turned into a night full of pain.

Lesson learned:

The lesson learned is to encourage all of God's chosen people to take heed to the warning in life that God provides for us. The bible teaches that warning comes before destruction, but how often do we listen and take heed to the warnings we receive? The problem is that most people are spooky and expect God to come down from heaven or speak from heaven to them personally in order for them to believe. When God sends warnings they come in subtle ways, in a still quiet voice. The only way you can hear Him speaking is to be quiet and listen. God is constantly speaking to us and desires to do so, however we're often so trapped in the emotions of what we are presently going through that we can't hear him or simply refuse to listen. The early signs show that this young man is not trustworthy and has no true commitment to either woman. A decision is required at this point, what will the decision be? Will the women realize that now is the time to wise up and move on, or will they stay despite the warning? Before answering this question, how many times have you been warned and you didn't listen?

~ ~ ~ ~ ~ ~ ~ ~ ~ ~ ~

Analogy: Caught Up With A Booty Call

A young man decides that he wants to go out and hang out with a friend. Friends end up in a small night club. This young man meets a nice young lady and

The Pain In Pleasure

decides to bring her home. Well, it's late and one of his main women lives in a 5-minute radius so he doesn't think much of this because he runs the risk of getting caught by his main lady but he invites her in anyway. Excited about the new lady he doesn't really think about the risk of getting caught. He normally calls and checks in with her before she goes to bed. He is so overtaken by the new girl and gives her all of his attention he decides not to call besides it's late. He invites the person into his private area and one thing leads to another and he has forgotten to put one of his main lady's to bed. Well, she decides to call and check on him. He answers the phone while the other lady is lying next to him. The two of them begin to talk and during the conversation the main lady detects something not sounding right so she decides to get off the phone. Not really thinking much of the matter, the young man goes on to entertain his new company. All of a sudden, the phone rings again and he looks at the clock and it's about 2:30 am. He then looks at the caller id and it's his main lady calling again. So now, he's feeling something is not adding up quite right. He immediately picks up the phone with his drowsy voice and says hello. Sharon says, "Hey, I can't sleep why don't you come over my house." Kerry instantly says he's too tired and besides it's late. Sharon decides that she will come over to his house. Kerry says no because he's tired and Sharon says okay. Kerry turns over and lays down hoping Sharon doesn't come over; about ten minutes pass by and there's a knock on the door. Kerry's heart drops because he knows Sharon has just busted him. Kerry ignores several knocks until his guest wakes up and asks, "Is someone knocking at your door?" Kerry says, "No, it must be someone next door." All of a sudden, the phone rings. Oh boy, Sharon tells him to come downstairs to open the door because she wants to come in. Well, Kerry goes on to say how tired and sleepy he is and that he doesn't feel like coming down stairs. The young lady, being a born detective, and by trade, asks, "Whose car is parked in your driveway?" Of course not thinking well in the intensity of the moment, Kerry pauses and says he doesn't know. At this time, Sharon is at the door knocking harder and yelling at the top of her lungs for Kerry, insisting on coming in. Kerry is constantly saying he

The Pain In Pleasure

is tired and doesn't want to be bothered which was completely out of character for him. Meanwhile, the other young lady now has gotten restless and wants him to do something or she is leaving. Kerry convinces her that Sharon is crazy and he doesn't know why she is over his house; she believes him and complies with him. At this point, he's caught in a bind and can't make a move other than to continue to tell Sharon, who was outside the door, that no one was there and that she was crazy for being out there at this hour. Needless-to-say, the young lady inside couldn't leave and Sharon, his steady women outside, wouldn't leave. Sharon decides that she would camp out and later discovered that she was so persistent about being sure that someone was really in the house that when she had to use the bathroom, she did it outside rather than leave because she wanted to ensure that her instincts were correct.

Lesson learned:

This analogy, just like the last one, shows that oftentimes, people do not take heed to the warnings God provides for us. Our flesh/carnality provides a system or network of distractions called pride or ego that trip us up from the start. The enemy of our soul helps provide distractions as well. The emotions that we suffer with, along with the distractions of the enemy, are a recipe for disaster. The decisions we make without including an all-knowing God puts us, and sometimes our entire family, in a very vulnerable state. This recipe I entitle The True Pain in Pleasure. I believe that it reverts back to the superego and the flesh. Often we don't like losing something or someone so we go into immediate denial about the truth. Look at the extreme that Sharon is willing to go to, in order to prove to herself that Kerry is really being unfaithful to her. She compromises her moral and ethical values by refusing to face all of the signs in front of her to the degree that she urinates outside on the ground. The persistence that she shows in her willingness to remain outside his door should have been used to distance herself from this scoundrel. The blinding affects of love causes people to lose focus of what God has clearly put before them. Kerry's booty call caused pain for the person who loved him dearly all because of his desire for a cheap thrill.

The Pain In Pleasure

Kerry's pleasure caused Sharon and the girl he met in the nightclub unnecessary pain.

~~~~~~~~~~

Analogy: Who's Got Game?

Playing the game is a very dangerous thing that a lot of people play growing up. No, I'm not talking about football or basketball, I'm talking about the games we play with relationships that aren't meaningful. You know, when you're just out to have some "innocent and harmless" fun with another person's emotions or feelings. The game is, you think I like you but in all actuality it's not you I like, it's what you have or what you can do for me that I really like. I like you enough to give you the time and the attention that you're seeking in order to get what you have. See, it's not about you or what you have to bring to the table in a relationship, it's all about me getting what I need from and out of you by any means necessary.

The "game" is a term used for playing or having fun in a relationship or several relationships. Who has the game in the relationship is very critical. See, what happens in some relationships is that both people don't have the same focus or agenda. There are so many hidden agendas going on with some people it takes years to discover them. In some relationships, we often have to fight through a lot of foolish issues and drama. All these issues sometimes have to be exposed before you can even begin to realize the person you're with 'got game.' The funny thing about it is you have no idea what his or her true intentions are.

~ ~ ~ ~ ~ ~ ~ ~ ~ ~

Analogy: The Gym Hook-Up

Tommy and Danielle see each other at the gym on a regular basis but they have never had a conversation. One day at Wal-Mart they recognize one another outside the gym setting and instantly become attracted to one another. They make eye contact and begin introducing themselves as seeing one another at the gym. The two have an instant connection toward each other. They both make mention of noticing how neither of them have ever spoken while in the gym. They both admit to noticing one another, although not speaking until now. He tells her he sees her working out with her boyfriend. She replies it's not her boyfriend but just a workout partner. Instantly

The Pain In Pleasure

they connect and feel more comfortable with moving forward. They both give the impression to one another that they are available to get involved. She also comments on why he always looks so mean while working out in the gym. They both laugh at the not so funny comment. He replies by saying that's just how he looks to keep the women from bothering him while working out. They laugh and continue to talk, really enjoying one another's conversation. So, they exchange numbers even though both of them are already involved with other people. The conversation never goes in that direction; in fact, it's not mentioned at all at this point.

They begin to talk on the phone and find out that they both have some common likes and dislikes. Neither has yet to reveal that they are seeing other people. They continue to see one another at the gym but now they are friendlier and they are chatting on the phone more. All of this conversation is constantly going on and nobody has said a word about their other relationship. This goes on for a while as they continue to stay in touch with one another. The relationship has now evolved into more than just the gym; they're hanging out at his house, doing dinner, etc. They played along with each other, not really making any decisions to go further, but not attempting to end anything either.

This sort of thing happens every day. A male or female decides what they have isn't really what they want and see something that looks like it could be or might be better than what they have and they go for it. This normally ends up in a lose-lose or a win-loss situation. A lose-lose situation is where neither one of them end up getting what they really want out of the relationship, but end up with pain and suffering. The pain of not getting what you expected to gain causes you to walk away very hurt. A win-loss is where one person appears to the other one as a winner, but it's just perception not reality.

To make a long story short, the relationship escalates into something neither one of them could ever imagine or they both end up hurt not to mention several other people who got caught up in the crossfire of the game over the years that this relationship went on. For

The Pain In Pleasure

example, Tommy and Danielle's boyfriend work at the same location. One day while at work, Tommy sees Danielle's car outside so he thinks she has popped up to surprise him while he's working overtime. Tommy sees someone standing at the car so he passes by only to see that Danielle is talking to his co- worker. Tommy makes sure they make eye contact with each other to ensure that she sees him while she is intimately engaged in the conversation with her live-in boyfriend. No, no confrontation happens. However, Danielle's live-in boyfriend, with great excitement, proceeds to discuss with Tommy his future plans with Danielle. Should Tommy be hurt? Should we feel sorry for Tommy? The answer to the questions is No. Tommy has a serious relationship that he is still involved in. Was Tommy hurt about the situation? Yes, because deep down inside of Tommy and his selfish ways, he thought she was really all his, therefore Tommy was devastated.

Lesson learned:

Who's got the game? They both had game and as a result, they experienced lots of pleasure, but they also suffered great pain in the loss of a relationship that started out with game.

See, what wasn't exposed in the beginning was that Danielle had a live-in boyfriend and Tommy was also already seriously involved with someone else. The two of them could have saved each other great measures of future pain, by being honest. This relationship started out being dishonest and they both knew it. They both had game but the relationship caused more pain and pleasure than most of the scenarios you have read thus far. Neither of them really looked to gain a long term or serious relationship from the other. They both saw something that they wanted for the time being, played with it, liked it, loved it, and in the end, couldn't keep it.

In life, it's challenging to have something you want so badly. Then you finally get an opportunity to have it for a while, but in the end you realize it can never really be yours. They both went into the game hoping to have fun, only to lose something they both loved in the end. The pain in the pleasure... Do you know what's ultimately behind your pleasures?

The Pain In Pleasure

Analogy: **Friends to the End**

    Hello Yvette, how are you and Charles doing? You know, Terry and I are having a house warming party on January 1st. No, I had no idea you guys had built a new home. I know Terry told Charles a couple of months ago. Girl, you know since y'all got married a couple of months ago, they haven't been running their mouths on the phone like two females. I know girl they are thick as thieves. I'm still surprised that we finally got them to settle down and marry us. The two of them have been the best of friends, doing dirt and chasing women for the last five years together. I know, Terry's toast as Charles' best man at our wedding said it all. Well, Charles didn't tell me girl but I will be there. Let me ask Charles if he can make it right now. Charles abruptly replies, "I can't make it." Teal says, "What? Terry is going to be devastated his best man isn't going to be here to celebrate with him." Teal says, "Girl, you know that's his only friend here."

    Three more weeks have passed and Charles calls Teal on the phone while she and Terry are driving to Burlington Coat Factory to look for items for the house.

Charles says, "Hello Teal, is Terry with you?" Teal says, "Yes, why didn't you call him on his phone?" Charles says, "I wanted to talk to you, but Terry's with you so I'll call you later." Teal says, "What?" Charles says, "That's okay. I'll talk to you later when Terry's not around." Teal hangs up and doesn't think anything of Charles' statement, "I'll call you when Terry's not around." One week away from the house warming party, Charles calls Teal while Terry's not around. "Hey Teal, this is Charles, I wanted to let you know that I would not be coming to your house warming party because I can't bear to be around Terry." Teal says, "What? I thought he was your best friend." Charles continues on to say, "I can't be around him knowing that he is cheating on you with Nikisha." Teal is shocked and speechless to hear Charles' statement that her new husband of three months is cheating on her, and for this to becoming from Terry's best friend, and now. Charles says, "Teal, I love you and I just can't be around Terry knowing what he is doing to you." Teal immediately hangs up the phone and calls Terry to confront him about what Charles just informed her. Teal

The Pain In Pleasure

further tells Terry the reason Charles is not coming is because he can't stand to be around him knowing that he is cheating on her. Terry is furious at Charles' allegations and immediately questions Charles' motives and reasoning for calling Teal. Neither Terry nor Teal can seem to figure out Charles' motive behind his attempt to ruin their marriage. Terry tells Teal that Charles has been rather distant since he shared the news of them moving into their new home three months ago. Terry says that the two of them have rarely talked in three months. They had seen each other once at the Best Buy when Nikisha and I ran into each other looking through DVDs on sale. He remembers Charles acting as if he really didn't want to speak to either of them, even though the three of them were all the best of friends. Terry says, "But even if what Charles is saying is true, then wouldn't it make more sense for him to confront me about these allegations, seeing how we're supposed to be best friends and all, rather than call my wife of three months? Then, if I continued to cheat on you despite his warning, I could understand him feeling justified in calling you with such devastating news. But, to call you with this and now…" "Terry, what are you going to do?" asked Teal. "Are you going to confront Charles about this?" Terry responds, "From this day forward, I hereby break my ties of five years with a friend that I considered my brother and my best friend until such a time as God sees fit to restore it."

Lesson learned:

In the bible, David and Jonathan had a bond and that bond was built on true brotherly love. A love, described like no other in the bible, of two natural non-related men before. Jonathan loved David so much that even though he was the true heir to the Kingdom he never allowed jealousy or greed to get in the way of their friendship. When King Saul, Jonathan's father, sought to kill David to prevent him from becoming king of Israel, it was Jonathan who warned David of his plan.

Here we have Terry and Charles, two friends who have been closer than natural brothers, whose friendship comes to an abrupt end and for what? What was Charles' motive for sharing this information? Was he attempting to destroy their marriage by sharing such devastating news with Teal, a wife of three months? The bible teaches us that

The Pain In Pleasure

what God has joined together let no man put asunder. The bible also says when you see a brother in sin, go to him in private and confront him about his sin. Praying for Terry and confronting him about what he thought was true, based on what he believed to be evidence, would have been a brotherly act. Am I my brother's keeper? Yes I am. Two men's lives shatter forever, and for what? Always seek God's guidance and instruction when making decisions that will affect the lives of the ones you love.

2 Timothy 3 2 Timothy 3:1-4 (Amplified Bible)

"BUT UNDERSTAND this, that in the last days will come (set in) perilous times of great stress and trouble [hard to deal with and hard to bear]."

"For people will be lovers of self and [utterly] self-centered, lovers of money and aroused by an inordinate [greedy] desire for wealth, proud and arrogant and contemptuous boasters. They will be abusive (blasphemous, scoffing), disobedient to parents, ungrateful, unholy and profane."

"[They will be] without natural [human] affection (callous

and inhuman), relentless (admitting of no truce or appeasement); [they will be] slanderers (false accusers, troublemakers), intemperate and loose in morals and conduct, uncontrolled and fierce, haters of good."

"[They will be] treacherous [betrayers], rash, [and] inflated with self-conceit. [They will be] lovers of sensual pleasures and vain amusements more than and rather than lovers of God."

The Pain In Pleasure

CHAPTER 6

Spiritually Blinded by Pleasures

Spiritually Blinded By Pleasures

Analogy: The Dirty Deacon

"Deacon Larry, I couldn't help but notice the argument you were having with Sister Smith. I believe it would be better for you both in the near future to have your heated arguments someplace other than the church's front parking lot. The both of you were extremely loud and used very harsh and inappropriate language toward one another. The verbal altercation that you were having was noticed by several other saints besides me. I don't know what's all going on, but Sister Smith seems to be extremely angry about the fact that you lied to her about sleeping with Brenda. She also appears to be disappointed about the four hundred dollars that she loaned you for your car payment six months ago and you have yet to make any arrangements or attempts to repay the money. The only reason I know this, Deacon Larry, is because like everyone else, I happened to hear the major altercation that you just had. In fact, I'm the one who called the police. When I called, I figured it was someone from the neighborhood arguing, fussing and fighting, not the deacon in the church."

"Deacon Larry, how is it that you go to church lifting up the name of Jesus and praising the Lord all the time and behave this way? Why is a direct representative of God and the church sleeping around with several different women? Deacon Larry, on top of that, you take money and gifts from these women. Deacon Larry you have to decide today who you love the most. Your fleshly desires have now openly caused you Pain in Pleasure ."

Lesson learned:

Matthew 6:24, "No one can **serve two masters**. Either he will hate the one and love the other, or he will be devoted to the one and despise the other. You cannot **serve** both God and Money."

The analogy you just read gives a clear indication that Deacon Larry has a very important decision he has to make. The Holy scriptures teach that God would rather his people be hot or cold and not lukewarm. If you are lukewarm, He will spew you out. Scripture teaches that we can only have one master. We live in a materialistic

The Pain In Pleasure

society where many people serve money and lustful desires. Lustful desires cause men to be lured into doing ungodly acts simply to please themselves. Ungodly pleasures do come with a high price. Money also causes men to spend their lives collecting and storing money, only to die and leave it behind.

The desire for money and what it can buy sometimes far outweighs man's commitment to God and spiritual matters. Whatever you store up, you will spend much of your time and energy thinking about. Don't fall into the materialistic trap, because the love of money is the root of all kinds of evil. Can you honestly say that, God and not money is your master? One test is to ask yourself which one occupies more of your thoughts, time and efforts.

Often in ministry, there are some good and bad representatives of Christ. Of course I completely understand growth and how God has us all in the refining process. How many times have you driven by a church and noticed the deacons outside the church smoking? This, in my opinion, is really a poor representation of a servant of God and the church. Often we, as so called Christians, forget who we represent. I state this based on the fact that when it comes to doing something that pleases ourselves or our flesh, we override the Holy Spirit and do that which is pleasing to us. We make this decision based on what our flesh dictates to us.

This chapter is called "The Dirty Deacon" not because all deacons are dirty, but because the deacon more commonly has a tendency to forget the vital responsibility their role calls for. This chapter will not just be about the deacon, but will focus on others in ministry as well, such as the ministers who misrepresent God by fulfilling their own desires. These desires are driven by various distractions; and these distractions are often driven by hidden motives, ungodly agendas, and evil forces at work against the vision and purpose of God. They also can be just pure selfish desires.

~~~~~~~~~~

Analogy: The bible teaches about being proven; meaning through our trials and experience we are tested. We must pass the test put before us. This analogy is about a young man who believes he truly loves God with all of his heart and

The Pain In Pleasure

soul. The problem is, he loves women and sex just as much. The young man is very deeply involved in ministry and is a wonderful help to the pastor and the people of God. The young man is not only young in body but in spiritual things as well. He doesn't truly understand the powerful enemy of his soul that he will have to face and overcome. Remember, the enemy deceives and covers up truth.

This young deacon begins to serve two masters without fully understanding what he is doing. This sort of thing happens in the Christian community often due to the lack of teaching as well as the lack of understanding of the true word of God. This young man goes on for years not realizing he is really just a pawn being used by the enemy. His mind is set to believe that as long as he consistently goes to church and praises God, that he is okay and God truly understands his heart. What he doesn't understand is that because of his decision, he is off track. The bible teaches that the heart is deceitful and desperately wicked. God will judge sin no matter how many excuses we have for why we do what we do. Proverbs 21:2, "All a man's way seem right to him, but the Lord weighs the heart."

Lesson learned:

The bible teaches that we must study to show ourselves approved, rightly dividing the word of truth. The bible also teaches that we must work out our own soul's salvation. The word of God is very clear and precise when it comes to God's expectation of His people. This information clearly indicates that it is necessary for me to have a deep personal relationship with Christ Jesus. Through my relationship with Him, He will reveal unto me my pathway.

The footsteps of a righteous man are ordered by the Lord. The Lord orders our footsteps under the operation of the Holy Spirit that He freely gives to His children for our success. When we walk after our own desires, God will turn us over to our own lusts. The young man in this analogy has allowed the enemy to deceive him. This young man, like many of today's Christians, believes that God is going to wink at sin; but God is a righteous judge and He will judge us according to His word. When God's children take His word and learn of Him, they will pass every test put before them, so we are

The Pain In Pleasure

without excuse. God clearly states that He is no respecter of persons, whatsoever a man sows that he shall also reap. God is going to judge His children more harshly because He states to whom much is given much is required.

Analogy: Pastor Stan

"Praise the Lord Pastor Stan. What got into you this morning? You gave me goose bumps with that powerful soul searching word. I really enjoyed the message. You had me right where I was in the world. I mean, I felt like you were speaking to me. Pastor, do you believe we can schedule some one-on-one counseling as soon as possible, because I don't want to hold the line up. I know all these people are trying to get to you as well as me. Besides, there are some things I just want to get off my chest. I'm sure you know just what I mean." "Why certainly, Sister Walker. I'm here to ensure that your needs are met. We can meet now if you like." That's just what I was hoping you would say Pastor Stan. Okay sister, let's go to my private study and there you can share with me whatever you have on your heart."

The women shares with the pastor that she is tired of being his chick on the side and demands that he leaves his wife or she is going to expose him for the real person he is, in front of his wife and his congregation. The two of them get involved in a heated argument over who's wrong and who's right. The pastor gets upset, he yells at the woman and tells her that he isn't threatened by her. The pastor further states that this is his church and his congregation and he tells her that she or no one else is going to remove him from the church. He further states to her that he has been to jail once and he isn't afraid to go back, so she had better get out of his _____ office. The women refuses to leave and reminds him of all the false promises that he made to her while on their overnight trips to Virginia Beach, Atlanta, New Orleans and California. She expresses to him of how his wife doesn't know how to satisfy him in the bedroom the way she does and never will. The woman further reminds him of their two year old son and that she will be making the first lady and his three other children aware of Stanford Lamont Jones, their baby they have together. Pastor Stan

The Pain In Pleasure

immediately slaps her on the face, pushes her out of his office and slams the door. She leaves screaming and crying, only to return with the police.

The church finds out about the pastor's affair in the newspaper, after he's arrested for assault. The congregation is now separated and confused as to what to do or how to carry on with this shocking news about their pastor. The deacons of the church take charge. They inform the congregation that Pastor Stan is not available for comment about these false allegations and that God knows Pastor Stan's heart. In the meantime, who do they follow? The pastor they have grown to love or Sister Walker's story? The Police did come and arrest the pastor for assault but Sister Walker could just be lying on their pastor. What will the members do? Leave the church? Will the Pastor now decide to step down until God sees fit to restore? Or will he remain, regardless of his lack of ability to lead by example.

Lesson learned:

God knows my heart! This is a very famous statement that most men and women make when sharing their personal issues. Individuals make this statement in life when they have no clear or rational reason to give about their irrational actions. For example, the mistakes that most Christians make are normally attributed to their lack of ability to be successful in weak areas. So we easily say, "God knows my heart." The bible teaches that none are perfect and that all have fallen short of the glory of God. However, that doesn't prevent or excuse Christians from striving for perfection. This statement of truth does not give man an opportunity to sin and continue in sin. The bible warns us, "Shall we continue in sin that grace may abound?" God forbid. All have sinned but Christians should not engage in willful sin, meaning sinning on purpose. The pastor in this analogy has been creeping sliding and has clearly lost focus on his mission of building the kingdom of God. Men and women in leadership have a huge obligation to God and His chosen people. Yes they are human, however they are more than conquers in Christ Jesus who strengths us all. God truly does know our hearts, however the problem comes in when we don't know our own hearts. The bible teaches us that the heart is wickedly deceitful and that is from where the issues of life flow. If the bible teaches that the heart is wickedly deceitful, then it could easily trick us couldn't it? The tricks are normally spilled out of the emotions that we suffer with on a day-to-day basis.

The intimate involvement of righteous leaders in the lives of young saints of God is necessary. The key component is righteousness. So often, we see many leaders who are not righteous and they have set many inappropriate examples for the body of Christ. A righteous leader leads by the guiding of the Holy Spirit and he or she knows the importance of teaching through application.

It's so amazing, how some people are more concerned with the leader's gender as opposed to their character. There is perhaps no more hotly debated issue in the church today than the issue of women serving as pastors/preachers. As a result, it is very important to not see this issue as men versus women. There are women who believe women should not serve as pastors and that the bible places restrictions on the ministry of women, and there are men who believe women can serve as preachers this is not an issue of chauvinism or discrimination. It is an issue of biblical interpretation. Shouldn't the decision be based on the leader's proven character and their proven ability to lead God's people by the voice of God? In this analogy like so many others, Pastor Stan is leading but setting a terrible example for Gods people. A leader should be an example by the leading of the Holy Spirit which is the voice of God rather than by their gender. Rather male or female God uses whomever He chooses to use for his glory. (1 Timothy 2:11-12) is the scripture that has caused various controversial interpretation over this very matter. The scriptures teach us that our people perish because of the lack of knowledge.

"So, since Christ suffered in the flesh for us, for you, arm yourselves with the same thought and purpose [patiently to suffer rather than fail to please God]. For whoever has suffered in the flesh [having the mind of Christ] is done with [intentional] sin [has stopped pleasing himself and the world, and pleases God]. So that he can no longer spend the rest of his natural life living by [his] human appetites and desires, but [he lives] for what God wills."

The Pain In Pleasure

"For the time that is past already suffices for doing what the Gentiles like to do—living [as you have done] in shameless, insolent wantonness, in lustful desires, drunkenness, reveling, drinking bouts and abominable, lawless idolatries."

CHAPTER 7

The Pains of Pleasure

The Pains of Pleasure

When the Ones I Love Don't Love Me Back

God, I love you with all my heart and it's my sincere desire to be pleasing to you. Often times, we ask the question, "Why is it that my greatest trial or challenges come from those closest to me?" The first thing that comes to mind is when the Apostle Paul gave reverence to the thorn in his side. This can give clear indication that your greatest pain or enemy could either be you or someone closest to you. When people think of their enemies, the last person they would expect are the ones who work closely with them like a wife or a mother. But remember, Job's wife tried to convince Job to curse God and die because she was blinded by the enemy or better yet, her lack of relationship with God caused her to not understand what God was doing with her husband and family. You might wonder why, Judas would walk so close with God but, in the end, betray God. This question is raised in the bible, "How can two walk together unless they agree?" Having vision is more than just being able to see what's in front of you.

Have you ever wondered what happens when you get a husband or wife who sees on different levels? I'll tell you, you have a couple who is unequally yoked; and what you do from there will determine the purpose and mission that God has for you. The enemy will take the person closest to you and blind them without warning. Now this is not a natural blinding but a spiritual blinding or dumbness. This act of the enemy is to bring a direct attack on the mission or purpose that God has for His people. Spiritual blindness comes in subtle ways and before you know it, the enemy has completely divided the family because of the mission that God has for them. Take Adam and Eve for example. The enemy came in and caused a split in the family, based on the influence that the wife and husband had on one another. The influence affects the entire family and could cause death, both naturally and spiritually.

Analogy: Unequally Yoked

A husband and wife have a different and unique relationship with God and everything appears to be going along well. God starts to use one more than the other,

The Pain In Pleasure

based on the one's obedience to God and His word. The other notices God is using their spouse a little more than them. He or she has a decision to make: "Will I seek God so that we may remain equally yoked and balanced as one in Christ Jesus, or will I be convinced by the enemy or the evil imagination?" God speaks and gives the answers we need, however, we decide in our hearts what we want. When what we want doesn't match what God speaks we don't accept it.

This agreement is just what the enemy wants and now he has you right where he wants you. This begins with small disagreements that have no real basis at all. Remember, the bible says it's the small foxes that destroy the vine. The vine now begins to be chipped away every time there is disagreement or a slight peak of jealousy. Disagreement doesn't always start out verbally. Many disagreements start in the heart. The verbal disagreement is readily noticed by a child of God, but the disagreement of the heart you can't always discern or detect right away. So, over a period of time, one will notice that there has been a major shift in the marriage that has caused some separation. Only God can provide the insight to notice and discern such a shift. This shift can happen without the slightest hint to the other spouse being made aware of it. This drifting away can go on for years before the spouse takes heed to the warnings God provides. Meanwhile, he or she is full of lustful desires for things or people, rather than the spouse that God gave them.

Putting lust to death is a must for the child of God. The Christian has to recognize that lust can and will rule your life. The reason we have to allow God to deliver us from these demonic forces is because it's controlling and outright nasty. You see, lust is like a drug. If you have ever dealt with lust, it can make you lose your mind. No, not literally, but it will cause you to do some very strange things… things you wouldn't normally do. Before you know it, you're completely out of control. Lust will cause you to start doing things you wouldn't normally do, but all of a sudden there you are, lowering your moral and ethical standards. This lust thing doesn't play fair, no matter who you are or your position—married or single. Lust can get your life out of control. This is one of the main statements that support "The Pain in Pleasure." Lust feels good but it's

The Pain In Pleasure

slowly killing you. Lust never lets you know that it is a slow killer.

Relationships should never be taken for granted. In each one, we should seek out its true purpose. Some relationships are designed to get you off your course. Some relationships are designed to destroy your marriages, homes, careers, etc. and before you recognize it, it's too late.

For example, I once met a wonderful female companion that I fell very much in love with. Things seemed to be so perfect. She appeared to be everything a man could ask for. Little did I know it was just lust operating. The relationship skyrocketed out of control. In the beginning, things were wonderful and we really enjoyed one another's company. Time eventually set in and what was once so lovely became extremely painful. I left some things out because I wanted you to fill in the blanks to this analogy with your personal testimony.

The pain was the result of the choices we both made, however, in the beginning, everything was rotated around the happiness of each other. Somewhere down the road that love quickly turned sour, similar to most of the analogies that I have pointed out in this book.

I hope that each reader recognizes for him or her self the distinct difference in their emotions before the pain sets in. In this book, my goal has been to get each reader to fully understand the pain in pleasure, and the cause and affects of both through various analogies.

I'm writing in the grace and love of my Lord and Savior, Jesus Christ. Through the enlightenment of the Holy Spirit, the Holy Scriptures, and other inspired writings my eyes have been open to, I credit Joe Beam, author of the book, "Seeing the Unseen," for his inspired work, research and the entire effort place in the book—both seen and unseen. Joe's research and inspired work opened my eyes to some very critical thinking and the need for some necessary changes in my spiritual life.

I grew up in a traditional church where some teaching went on, but there was more hooping and yelling that took place on Sunday morning, rather than the teaching of sound doctrine. I believe this sort of emotional church has caused a rift in many individuals receiving and

The Pain In Pleasure

accepting sound spiritual bible-based teaching in our churches today. There is still today so many different interpretations or, better yet, opinions about whether a woman should be in leadership as a pastor or any other high-ranking positions in the church. Much of this thinking derived from inappropriate teaching of the bible. There is one scripture, that I know of, that supports this theory. However, if you read the chapter before and after, it gives the rationale behind what has been a thorn in the side of many people today. Research shows that most people strongly believe that Sunday morning messages should be motivational but not without sound bible-based teaching. Preachers should be motivational, but some are more theatrical than instructional and people are drowning as a result of an emotional high that leaves them as soon as they exit the church pew. This is still happening in churches today, across the world and in various races and cultures as well. The preacher is yelling and screaming and the people are appearing to enjoy and even loving it, but what are they really learning? What I have learned from this experience is that people often want to get their emotions pleased. The preacher, rather than seek God for a true word that will cause a change in the lives of the people, instead plays on the emotions of the congregation. They jump up and down and on top of chairs and pews; some yell at the top of their voices. All along, the congregation sits in support of this type of false entertainment while their souls suffer from the lack of knowledge. It's not my desire to judge or condemn. However, I have experienced many emotional highs throughout my 23 years of salvation and I have talked to people who were extremely excited during service but directly afterwards, they can't tell you what the title or scripture of the message was. The bible teaches that as soon as the word goes out, Satan comes immediately to take it back or to come against it so that the hearer doesn't retain it. However, it's critically important to know and protect the word of God that we receive. I believe that a lot of preachers mean well but they have been taught wrong or haven't been taught at all, or it could be they are patterning themselves after what they have seen and believe to be appropriate. The bible teaches us that the people perish because of the lack

The Pain In Pleasure

of knowledge. The bible also teaches that we have to study to show ourselves approved, rightly dividing the word of truth. God's word teaches that He will not have us ignorant concerning His word. When we hear the word and know the word in our hearts, we won't sin against God. It is extremely important for us to know the word of God in order to avoid the pitfalls of life.

The people must be taught how to live out the scriptures in a victorious way. Entertainment has its place, but it should never take the place of the word of God. The word, with application, causes a lifestyle of trusting, believing and living out the word of God. A victorious Christian lifestyle is proven through application, and demonstration. It's line upon line, and precept upon precept. Some preachers put on a show. God forbid that the preacher can sing. That's all he does when he should be teaching. Don't get me wrong, I love singing but I want to learn about God's word and how to live for God; not see a talent show. Many of these talent shows are forced upon us. And we are not always inspired by the Holy Spirit. Many have been going on for years and people have grown to love them and actually like to see it. Well my friend, I'm here to tell you it's a trick of the enemy. People like to see things or be involved in things that solely entertain them like the movies, American Idol or America's Got Talent. Today, there are more reality shows on TV than ever before in history. The church isn't exempt from this or any other problem that the world faces. If we are properly taught within our churches, we would be better equipped to deal with the things this world presents to us. Otherwise, we just do what seems right to us. I believe these are some of the reasons we, as the people of God, suffer through the pains of our ungodly pleasures.

The Bible teaches us that men will become lovers of themselves. The view of the world today shows the "dog eat dog" world in which we live. Society concerns itself with "me" "my" and "I" syndrome. The bible speaks about how men will lust after their own desires and forget about God. This has already started to happen in pulpits around America. Yes, pulpits that don't have God at the center. When Jesus left this world, He said that He would not leave us comfortless, so He left us with the Holy Spirit to guide us

The Pain In Pleasure

on earth. The Holy Spirit is a free gift from God for all born again believers. But all don't choose to receive this wonderful gift of the Holy Spirit and some have it, but they don't release it to have full control in their lives. God knew we would need it, so He left it for us. Will you let the Holy Spirit lead and guide you today; and to steer you away from the pain and sufferings that are brought about by your lustful drive?

CHAPTER 8
Theory vs. Scripture

The Pain In Pleasure

Theory vs. Scripture
(Snowden, Ruth. Teach Yourself Freud.
New York, Mcgraw-Hill, 2006).

The goal here is to offer the reader an opportunity to view additional sources in order to gain a clear and precise understanding of "The Pain in Pleasure." The pain in pleasure is something that we don't often recognize immediately or on our own. Sometimes, people need to seek professional as well as spiritual help. I believe that by involving both it will enhance and broaden each reader's knowledge level. I know that by including well-noted theories by Sigmund Freud, and bible-based principles, I can and will accomplish my goal.

Through the next few pages, I believe your thoughts will be provoked—provoked to think about how pleasure works and how you have perceived it to work for years. The psychoanalytic concepts may startle you a little, as well as give you a better understanding of how your mind and thoughts can work for or against you.

This research is not my own but that of pioneers who have paved the way for those of us who desire to have a better understanding of how we think, based on proven research.

id, **ego**, and **super-ego** are the three parts of the psychic apparatus defined in Sigmund Freud's structural model of the psyche; they are the three theoretical constructs in terms of whose activity and interaction mental life is described. According to this model, the uncoordinated instinctual trends are the "id;" the organized realistic part of the psyche is the "ego;" and the critical and moralizing function is the "super-ego."

Id

The id comprises the unorganized part of the personality structure that contains the basic drives. The id acts as according to the "pleasure principle," seeking to avoid pain or displeasure aroused by increases in instinctual tension. The id is unconscious by definition. In Freud's formulation,

Ego

The ego comprises that organized part of the personality structure that includes defensive, perceptual,

The Pain In Pleasure

intellectual-cognitive, and executive functions. Conscious awareness resides in the ego, although not all of the operations of the ego are conscious. The ego separates what is real. It helps us to organize our thoughts and make sense of them and the world around us.

According to Freud...

In Freud's theory, the ego mediates among the id, the super-ego and the external world. Its task is to find a balance between primitive drives and reality (the Ego devoid of morality at this level) while satisfying the id and super-ego. Its main concern is with the individual's safety and allows some of the id's desires to be expressed, but only when consequences of these actions are marginal. Ego <u>defense mechanisms</u> are often used by the ego when id behavior conflicts with reality and either society's morals, norms, and taboos or the individual's expectations as a result of the internalization of these morals, norms, and their taboos.

When the ego is personified, it is like a slave to three harsh masters: the id, the super-ego, and the external world. It has to do its best to suit all three, thus it is constantly feeling hemmed by the danger of causing discontent on two other sides. It is said, however, that the ego seems to be more loyal to the id, preferring to gloss over the finer details of reality to minimize conflicts while pretending to have a regard for reality. But the super-ego is constantly watching every one of the ego's moves and punishes it with feelings of <u>guilt</u>, <u>anxiety</u>, and inferiority. To overcome this the ego employs <u>defense mechanisms</u>. The defense mechanisms are not done so directly or consciously. They lessen the tension by covering up our impulses that are threatening.

Denial, displacement, intellectualization, projection, fantasy, compensation, rationalization, reaction formation, regression, repression, and sublimation were the defense mechanisms Freud identified. However, his daughter, <u>Anna Freud</u>, clarified and identified the concepts of undoing, suppression, dissociation, summarization, idealization, identification, introjections, inversion, splitting, and substitution.

Super-ego

The super-ego aims for perfection. It comprises that organized part of the personality structure, mainly but not entirely unconscious, that includes the individual's <u>ego ideals</u>, spiritual goals, and the psychic agency (commonly called "conscience") that criticizes and prohibits his or her drives, fantasies, feelings, and actions.

The super-ego works in contradiction to the id. The super-ego strives to act in a socially appropriate manner, whereas the id just wants instant self-gratification. The super-ego controls our sense of right and wrong and guilt. It helps us fit into society by getting us to act in socially acceptable ways.

The super-ego's demands oppose the id's, so the ego has a hard time in reconciling the two. Freud's theory implies that the super-ego is a symbolic internalization of the <u>father figure</u> and cultural regulations. The super-ego tends to stand in opposition to the desires of the id because of their conflicting objectives, and its aggressiveness towards the ego. The super-ego acts as the <u>conscience</u>, maintaining our sense of morality and proscription from taboos.

Scripture vs. Theory was simply to give you some background on the pleasure principles that Sigmund Freud's research discovered. Freud's work was very significant in this research to provide the natural occurrence of behavior based on what you have read and perhaps understood about the pleasure principle. Paul on the other hand has provided some very in depth spiritual insight on the pleasures that we face and how to overcome them. Supernatural is a very complex topic for some Christian and non Christians as well. The supernatural deals with things seen as well as things not seen. The pain in pleasures is rotated around things or forces of the unseen. Things that are perhaps lustful in nature like our desires, urges and pleasures in life that happens to have strong controlling power over us.

Why Do We Do What We Do?

2 Corinthians 10:3-10 (Amplified Bible)

"For though we walk (live) in the flesh, we are not carrying on our warfare according to the flesh and using mere human weapons. For the weapons of our warfare are not physical [weapons of flesh and blood], but they are mighty before God for the overthrow and destruction of strongholds, [Inasmuch as we]

The Pain In Pleasure

refute arguments and theories and reasoning's and every proud and lofty thing that sets itself up against the [true] knowledge of God; and we lead every thought and purpose away captive into the obedience of Christ (the Messiah, the Anointed One),

Why do we do what we do? The scriptures you just read give an outline of how the child of God operates which is contrary to what Freud talked about in the pleasure principles as it relates to the id, ego, and super ego. Freud gives a natural theoretical terminology on why we do what we do, based on the pleasure principle expressed through the id ego and super ego. The reason for sharing with you in detail Freud's Pleasure Principle expressed though the id ego and super ego was to provide each reader and opportunity to grasp a better understand of God's word by comparing theory and Scripture.

God and His divine wisdom is expressed to His children through His written word. The written word of God gives us a deeper connotation of the spirit vs. flesh and the warfare that we endure. The scriptures express to us that our weapons are not carnal, physical or even mental as Freud would have us to believe but that of the spiritual realm. I believe that Freud provides an excellent natural and theoretical explanation for why we suffer through so many drastic changes in life. I agree with Freud and most of his theories about our egos because they are mentioned in the bible but with a different name. The bible speaks about our pride which correlates to our egos that Freud research supports. The ego, or our pride, causes us to make dreadful mistakes in life over and over again. One would think that it's like self-mutilation when we constantly do the same things over and over again as expressed through the analogies you have read. A famous quote states that if you always do, what you have always done, you will always get what you've always got," the same results. The challenge here is to seek to have a closer relationship with God, and to allow Him to transform us through the renewing of our minds.

    Why do we do what we do? This question, when asked will generate various responses. Some responses will sound logical and others will not. The character expressing this statement, however, believes at least for that moment, that they have given a justifiable response. The Christian believer should have a profound understanding of God's word along with the operation of the Holy Spirit when he or she answers this question. The purpose for explaining or describing the type of Christian believer I'm talking about is because many professed Christians lack the obedience to God along with the operation of the Holy Spirit.

The various chapters analogies, theories and scriptures hopefully have convinced each reader to obey God's word no matter what their feelings or emotions might dictate to them. When researching the scriptures, as God has requested in His word that we do, study to show thyself approved, rightly dividing the word of truth. This statement should stimulate us to seek out the word of God for direction and instruction in our God-given purpose, and His principles according to the issues of life that we face and endure. God has blessed us with His inspired and Holy Word to help us make it through this journey called life.

Please read this next text of scripture very carefully.

Romans 8 (Amplified Bible)

"THEREFORE, [there is] now no condemnation (no adjudging guilty of wrong) for those who are in Christ Jesus, who live [and] walk not after the dictates of the flesh, but after the dictates of the Spirit."

As Christians we are not to be controlled by the flesh. Yes, we face the same challenges that every other human being faces. The difference is the id; ego, or super ego expressed in Freud's theory does not dominate or dictate to the child of the highest God. The children of God, through the obedience of God's commands, are given power to overcome those demands of the flesh by the power of the blood of Jesus. Please read on in Romans.

"For the law of the Spirit of life [which is] in Christ Jesus [the law of our new being] has freed me from the law of sin and of death."

"For God has done what the Law could not do, [its power] being weakened by the flesh the entire nature of

man without the Holy Spirit]. Sending His own Son in the guise of sinful flesh and as an offering for sin, [God] condemned sin in the flesh [subdued, overcame, deprived it of its power over all who accept that sacrifice]."

The scriptures here express how the child of God is more than capable of being victorious over the things of the flesh. Therefore the analogies that you have read and the ones you have lived are all in vein and unnecessary. These things are deemed unnecessary to go through when you are a true heir to the throne. There is no power greater than the power of God. There therefore no condemnation for those who are in Christ Jesus. God so loved the world that He gave His only begotten son that we might be saved through Him. The power to overcome every sin that so easily besets us has been provided through the blood of Jesus. Please continue to read this chapter for the clarity and understanding that God has supplied.

"So that the righteous and just requirement of the Law might be fully met in us who live and move not in the ways of the flesh but in the ways of the Spirit [our lives governed not by the standards and according to the

dictates of the flesh, but controlled by the Holy Spirit]. "For those who are according to the flesh and are controlled by its unholy desires set their minds on and pursue those things which gratify the flesh, but those who are according to the Spirit and are controlled by the desires of the Spirit set their minds on and seek those things which gratify the [Holy] Spirit."

"Now the mind of the flesh [which is sense and reason without the Holy Spirit] is death [death that] comprises all the miseries arising from sin, both here and hereafter]. But the mind of the [Holy] Spirit is life and [soul] peace [both now and forever]."

"[That is] because the mind of the flesh [with its carnal thoughts and purposes] is hostile to God, for it does not submit itself to God's Law; indeed it cannot."

"So then those who are living the life of the flesh [catering to the appetites and impulses of their carnal nature] cannot please or satisfy God, or be acceptable to Him."

"But you are not living the life of the flesh, you are living the life of the Spirit, if the [Holy] Spirit of God [really] dwells within you [directs and controls you]. But if anyone *does not possess the [Holy] Spirit of Christ, he is none of His [he does not belong to Christ, is not truly a child of God]."*

"But if Christ lives in you, [then although] your [natural] body is dead by reason of sin and guilt, the spirit is alive because of [the] righteousness [that He imputes to you]."

"And if the Spirit of Him Who raised up Jesus from the dead dwells in you, [then] He Who raised up Christ Jesus from the dead will also restore to life your mortal (short-lived, perishable) bodies through His Spirit Who dwells in you."

"So then, brethren, we are debtors, but not to the flesh [we are not obligated to our carnal nature], to live [a life ruled by the standards set up by the dictates] of the flesh."

"For if you live according to [the dictates of] the flesh, you will surely die. But if through the power of the [Holy] Spirit you are [habitually] putting to death (making extinct, deadening) the [evil] deeds prompted by the body, you shall [really and genuinely] live forever."

"For all who are led by the Spirit of God are sons of God. For [the Spirit which] you have now received [is] not a spirit of slavery to put you once more in bondage to fear, but you have received the Spirit of adoption [the Spirit producing son ship] in [the bliss of] which we cry, Abba (Father)! Father!"

"The Spirit Himself [thus] testifies together with our own spirit, [assuring us] that we are children of God."

"And if we are [His] children, then we are [His] heirs also: heirs of God and fellow heirs with Christ [sharing His inheritance with Him]; only we must share His suffering if we are to share His glory."

"[But what of that?] For I consider that the sufferings of this present time (this present life) are not worth being compared with the glory that is about to be revealed to us and in us and for us and conferred on us!"

"For [even the whole] creation (all nature) waits expectantly and longs earnestly for God's sons to be made known [waits for the revealing, the disclosing of their son ship]."

"For the creation (nature) was subjected to frailty (to futility, condemned to frustration), not because of

The Pain In Pleasure

some intentional fault on its part, but by the will of Him Who so subjected it--[yet] with the hope)."

"That nature (creation) itself will be set free from its bondage to decay and corruption [and gain an entrance] into the glorious freedom of God's children."

"We know that the whole creation [of irrational creatures] has been moaning together in the pains of labor until now."

"And not only the creation, but we ourselves too, who have and enjoy the first fruits of the [Holy] Spirit [a foretaste of the blissful things to come] groan inwardly as we wait for the redemption of our bodies [from sensuality and the grave, which will reveal] our adoption (our manifestation as God's sons)."

"For in [this] hope we were saved. But hope [the object of] which is seen is not hope. For how can one hope for what he already sees?"

"But if we hope for what is still unseen by us, we wait for it with patience and composure."

"So too the [Holy] Spirit comes to our aid and bears us up in our weakness; for we do not know what prayer to offer nor how to offer it worthily as we ought, but the

Spirit Himself goes to meet our supplication and pleads in our behalf with unspeakable yearnings and groanings too deep for utterance."

"And He Who searches the hearts of men knows what is in the mind of the [Holy] Spirit [what His intent is], because the Spirit intercedes and pleads [before God] in behalf of the saints according to and in harmony with God's will."

"We are assured and know that God being a partner in their labor] all things work together and are [fitting into a plan] for good to and for those who love God and are called according to [His] design and purpose."

"For those whom He foreknew [of whom He was] aware and [loved beforehand], He also destined from the beginning [foreordaining them] to be molded into the image of His Son [and share inwardly His likeness], that He might become the firstborn among many brethren."

"And those whom He thus foreordained, He also called; and those whom He called, He also justified (acquitted, made righteous, putting them into right

standing with Himself). And those whom He justified, He also glorified [raising them to a heavenly dignity and condition or state of being]."

"What then shall we say to [all] this? If God is for us, who [can be] against us? [Who can be our foe, if God is on our side?]"

"He who did not withhold or spare [even] His own Son but gave Him up for us all, will He not also with Him freely and graciously give us all [other] things?"

"Who shall bring any charge against God's elect [when it is] God Who justifies [that is, Who puts us in right relation to Himself? Who shall come forward and accuse or impeach those whom God has chosen? Will God, Who acquits us?]"

"Who is there to condemn [us]? Will Christ Jesus (the Messiah), Who died, or rather Who was raised from the dead, Who is at the right hand of God actually pleading as He intercedes for us?"

"Who shall ever separate us from Christ's love? Shall suffering and affliction and tribulation? Or calamity and distress? Or persecution or hunger or destitution or peril or sword?"

"Even as it is written, For Thy sake we are put to death all the day long; we are regarded and counted as sheep for the slaughter."

"Yet amid all these things we are more than conquerors and gain a surpassing victory through Him Who loved us."

"For I am persuaded beyond doubt (am sure) that neither death nor life, nor angels nor principalities, nor things impending and threatening nor things to come, nor powers, nor height nor depth, nor anything else in all creation will be able to separate us from the love of God which is in Christ Jesus our Lord."

I pray that after reading these powerful scriptures, every reader gains a better understanding of natural and spiritual things. I believe that God has given us a wonderful opportunity to be victorious in everything. God's word is truly like a lamp unto our feet. If we follow God's word, then truly our footsteps will be ordered by Him.

The Pain In Pleasure

These are the three components Freud believed that stimulated ones behavior, the Id, Ego, and Super-ego. He believed that this stimulated our behavior based on the psychoanalytical make up of our mind/intellect. I believe by reading this detail information about the Id, Ego and Super Ego shows the internal conflict according to Freud's Theory. Research shows that there is constant conflict between the three in making decisions based upon the moral, ethical, and spiritual issues of life.

In reading the Pain in Pleasure it reveals many analogies rotated around our choices in life and the effects that they have on us and our love ones. The struggles we face with the moral, ethical and spiritual components have been somewhat omitted and replaced with the word of God. This was done purposefully to institute or build on the existing relationship with God. I believe that if you are reading this book and you have made it this for there must be some form of knowledge about who God is. The word of God brings light where there is darkness. The purpose for sharing this information now is to correlate the natural being theory compared to the supernatural which is the word of God.

Our world today has supplied so many excuses as to why people do what they do. For instance there are so many different acronyms and labels place on people today. These acronyms begin with ADD attention deficit disorder, ADHD attention deficit hyperactive disorder or Bi-Polar. These are just some of the labels used today as to define why we make the decisions we make. Most people choose to accept this label rather than accept the fact that we simply need a closer relationship with Christ Jesus in our life. A life with Christ allows us the opportunity to receive complete deliverance. I do believe Freud had a very clear and vivid understanding of the perplexity of the mind based on his theoretical concept of the Id, Ego, and Super -ego. However I believe that Freud only dealt with the surface level. Spiritually we wrestle not with flesh and blood but with Principalities in high places. This means we deal with more than just the struggle of Good vs. Evil but demon forces and interferences.

I pray that after reading all of the analogies, lesson learned, and theories by Freud that you were not to over taken by them. Often times we try and rationalize why

The Pain In Pleasure

people do what they do without gaining true wisdom. Do you believe that we do what we do just because we want to without any support from evil forces or demonic activity? Being born in a world of sin automatically makes us a product of our environment; you add shapened in iniquity and were guaranteed to fail. Understanding this process alone provides a gateway for destruction unless we choose Jesus Christ as our personal savior.

Analog: Revenge How Sweet It Is... Or Is It?

Ring, Ring, Ring, Hello may I speak to Cornell? Cornell is in the shower, May I Ask Who Is Calling? Who is this? Who is this? This is Cornell's girlfriend if you must know! Cornell's girlfriend, well you tell him to call Valerie as soon as he gets out of the shower. Click! Oh, I know Cornell ain't got this chick up in his house hanging up the phone in my face. That's Cool she will get hers, trust and believe that.

Cornell gets out of the shower and immediately with an attitude Tracey says, "Cornell your phone was ringing while you were in the shower" Cornell says, "Ok" with little or no concern at all. Tracey then makes sure she lets Cornell know exactly what Valerie said," Valerie said, "you need to call her" Cornell says, "how do you know?" Tracey says, I know because I answered your telephone while you were in the shower," Cornell why is you still dealing with her?" Cornell then says, "Girl please you know we just friends." Yeah right! Tracey leaves extremely upset and goes home.

A few hours' later Valerie calls back and convinces Cornell of how much she misses him and wants to see him. Cornell quickly agrees and Valerie comes over. Once Valerie arrives one thing leads to another and shortly after their romantic encounter Cornell falls into a deep sleep on the floor.

Ring, Ring, Ring Cornell phone rings at 11:30 pm Valerie quickly answers the phone. Wow its Tracey and she is immediately shocked that another women is answering her man's phone and at this hour. Tracey knows, Cornell doesn't allow anyone to answers his phone without catching and attitude even with her. Tracey recognizes that the voice is the same voice from earlier this evening the person who she hung the phone up on.

The Pain In Pleasure

Valerie the women Cornell has been seeing, but denying. Valerie recognizes its Tracey and remembers how she hung up the phone on her earlier that evening. Valerie says Cornell is sleep. Click! Valerie hangs up the phone in Tracey's face. Tracey immediately calls back; Valerie answers the phone again laughing in the phone this time before hanging up. Tracey continues to call so Valerie unplugs the phone to keep Cornell from waking up to the sound of the phone ringing. Several hours go by before Valerie plugs the phone back up. The Phone immediately start ringing which clearly indicates, Tracey has been up all night calling Cornell's phone and didn't get any sleep at all. The phone continues to ring constantly until Cornell finally hears the phone and wakes up to answer it. Tracey is going off on the other end of the phone; Cornell who is barely awake lays the phone down out of frustration to her yelling in his ear. Valerie kisses Cornell tells him she loves him and leaves so Tracey can continue to confront Cornell. Meanwhile she leaves Cornell on the phone with Tracey who is furious because she has been calling his house since 11:30 pm and now its 4:00 am.

Lesson learned:

So what stimulated their behavior was there a struggle between the Id, Ego, and Super Ego as to whom to please or did they each experience a unique level of pain in this analogy or was it some demonic forces operating to promote this unkind act. Often people are motivated to do evil things based on the thoughts or evil imagination that Satan (The Devil) provide. Satan is a seducer who tempts the flesh so that people will engage in the pleasures of sin, these pleasures only last for a season. Satan along with his devils tries to draw people away from the word of God and towards all forms of wickedness. When we do unclean things or even think unclean thoughts, we open the door for Satan to get an advantage over us. This advantage is gained when people who are overly indulged in lustful wickedness within their minds. Unclean wicked things such as pornography, TV, movies, secular (or any kind of romance) books, lasciviousness, filthy communications and music, filthy friends, etc. All give an open door to the devil. The flesh is weak so if you are a Christian, you must mortify the deeds of your body. Masturbation and all unclean things are openings.

The Pain In Pleasure

The bible speaks about how evil communication corrupts good manner. The spirit truly is ready, but the flesh is weak. One thing the bible talks about is crucifying the flesh. When we crucify our flesh and focus on what God has in stored for us we can win. Our strength is in the full armor of God. The bible teaches that we should let this mind be in me that was also in Christ Jesus. Meaning I have to learn how to train my mind to think like Jesus. For our struggle is not against flesh and blood but against the rulers, against the authorities, against the powers of this dark world and against the spiritual forces of evil in the heavenly realm Ephesians 6: 12-13.

Spiritual warfare takes us into an arena of conflict with which most of us are not comfortable. We feel unprepared to do battle at this level. This is why we need biblical guidelines. The Apostle Paul urges us to stand firmly in the strength the Lord provides, wearing the armor that comes from God. Prayer strengthens us for the conflict so we can proclaim God's message without being permanently hindered by the enemy. Please read this scripture below and examine your life and the choices you have made in your body and even in your mind.

Galatians 5:16-17 (Amplified Bible)

"But I say, walk and live [habitually] in the [Holy] Spirit [responsive to and controlled and guided by the Spirit]; then you will certainly not gratify the cravings and desires of the flesh (of human nature without God)."

"For the desires of the flesh are opposed to the [Holy] Spirit, and the [desires of the] Spirit are opposed to the flesh (godless human nature); for these are antagonistic to each other [continually withstanding and in conflict with each other], so that you are not free but are prevented from doing what you desire to do."

Theory in my opinion now goes out the window. The bible states in 1 Peter 5:8 that Satan is like a roaring lion, looking for someone to devour. We must take our enemy Satan seriously because he has great power. Yet not too seriously, because he is a defeated foe. Please don't forget that we struggle against the world and the flesh as well as the Devil. Life truly is about choices and our responses to life's experience. Because you have been reading the pain in pleasure you should know that evil has a subtle way of looking likes it's not that harmful or it's ok.

The Pain In Pleasure

Each one of us walking this earth is involved with a spiritual battle. People will either walk after the Spirit of God or after the corrupted flesh. If we walk after the flesh Satan will have his way with us. At first it will seem pleasant, but then the flesh becomes addicted to lust doing stranger and stranger things. For example there are many different analogies you have been exposed to in this book alone. The analogies perhaps provided you with a source of entertainment but the thoughts and deeds were evil. The Bible calls it witchcraft. There is a solution to our problems and dilemmas found in Christ Jesus. If you are not saved all you have to do is accept Jesus Christ in your heart as your personal savior, believe that he died for the sins of this world and that he shall return. Now take time and learn of Jesus. Build a personal relationship with Him. Find you a bible believing, Spirit-filled Church and learn of him. Please read this next scripture and learn to live by.

2 Chronicles 7:14 (Amplified Bible)
"If My people, who are called by My name, shall humble themselves, pray, seek, crave, and require of necessity My face and turn from their wicked ways, then will I hear from heaven, forgive their sin, and heal their land."

Inventory Aptitude Test — Theory vs. Scriptures

My attitude toward the world's design for me is this:

- At this time, I am more in synchronization with the world than with God.
- I am tempted by all that the world has to offer.
- Although tempted, I am experiencing increasing victory over the world.
- The world holds little appeal to me as I meditate on all Christ has done for me.
- I am experiencing regular victory over the world.
- Life is what you make of it and no one is going to give me anything.

My attitude toward God's will for my life is this:

- Right now I am absorbed with my own plans.
- God knows my heart.
- I am increasingly aware of God's will and have a desire to do it.
- I want to follow God, although I am occasionally drawn back to my own way.
- God's will is where I want to be, but I'm not 100 percent there yet.
- I'm walking boldly in my destiny.
- I feel that I am living in the center of God's will for me.

The Pain In Pleasure

My View Regarding Spiritual Gifts:

- I do not know what my spiritual gift is and I don't care.
- I don't believe in spiritual gifts.
- I've heard about spiritual gifts, but I've never taken a spiritual gifts inventory.
- I have taken an inventory, but I didn't like what it showed.
- Things of the spirit are spooky and it scares me.
- I have begun to experiment with Christianity with Christian service in my area of spiritual giftedness.
- I am finding great fulfillment in serving Christ Through my spiritual gifts.

CHAPTER 9

The Purpose and Power of the Blood of Christ

The Purpose and Power of the Blood of Christ

When someone is so use to doing what they want to do, and how they want to do it, and they make their life decisions based on what makes them feel good, destruction is quickly coming around the corner. This is especially true when that's what you have grown accustomed to doing and have been doing all of your life. Change has now become almost impossible and would be very uncomfortable. So now who is in control, you or your flesh or should I say your lustful desires? Would you like to know why? Well I'm glad you asked. There's a war going on between our flesh and our spirit every day. You asked how? Good question, the bible teaches us that the spirit and the flesh are constantly at war against one another.

Okay, so you say prove it to me so I can clearly see what you're talking about. I will make every attempt to convince you of this theory. I will make this attempt by providing you with real life analogies and examples with hope that God will open your understanding and cause every reader to be convinced based on the principles of God.

Analogy:

In living your life, your body, which equals your flesh, has dictated to you all your life! It tells you when to eat and when to sleep; your body also tells you when you're tired. It tells you what you should do for it each day. Your body will say to you that it deserves this because: *I work hard. I don't want to read the word of God. I don't feel like exercising, I should have what I want. I don't want to fast; I don't want to worship God today. I don't have time for God.* Are you starting to see my point now? You're probably wondering why he feels he has to pull out these points about me. What makes him the expert, he thinks he knows it all. Understand these principles are based on the word of God and I challenge you to accept and research the scriptures.

These are just some examples of how we are before we see the true light of the world. We often rationalize why we do what we do, without any real responsibility to God for the things we do. Some of us only look to please and gratify our flesh. Listen, I know this to be true. I'm talking from experience because my flesh has controlled a

The Pain In Pleasure

large percentage of my life. My excuse was ignorance because I didn't fully understand the things of the spirit. Now I know God holds me fully responsible for my actions and the deeds that I do in this body I call my own. The actions and deeds I do in this body, that God has given me, are now re-focused toward God's purpose for my life. Is there still residue of evil inside of me even though I recognize that my body is not my own? Yes there is. The body that we have is supposed to be holy and acceptable unto God as my reasonable service. The need for constant deliverance for Christians becomes more necessary as we increase in wisdom and knowledge of God's word and purpose for our lives. Can I continue in sin that grace may abound? God forbid.

My spirit has suffered greatly as a result of the choices that I have made based on what I believe to be true or just on what felt good or right to me at the time. My spirit, along with the love of God, tells me I should not lust with my eyes, heart, or even in my mind. As you can see there is a contradiction between the spirit and the flesh. As men, we are very visual. When we see something appealing to us we usually want it. As a Christian man striving to live a life after Christ, I must discipline myself not to act on my foolish lustful desires. These desires only work to keep me bound in my sins, especially those sins that so easily beset me or get me caught up. In this last analogy, I pray that you will see the error of your ways. Based on the information shared in this final attempt, I hope it will persuade every reader to see and understand that the wages of sin is death. The pain in pleasure can and will be prevented by choosing God's ways and not man's. Some sins so easily beset us and trip us up but because we're so accustomed to doing things according to the ways of the world, we simply don't recognize that we are dying. I pray that you will read carefully this last analogy and see just how easy we fall into sin.

Analogy: A man is walking in the mall minding his own business, looking for something special for his wife; he doesn't plan on being in the mall long at all. All of a sudden, out of the left corner of his eyes, he sees this beautiful woman. Normally he looks and keeps it moving. Today he decides to look and stare... as he stares. He notices that she is everything physically that his wife is not or that her physical

The Pain In Pleasure

appearance is worth sacrificing his vows and even his marriage. His flesh appeals to his senses so in his mind, he rationalizes why he should pursue her. His eyes, mind, and flesh agree that she should have been his wife. His thoughts now have shifted from evil imagination to lustful desires, thinking about her in ways that he should be thinking about his own wife! Wow, so he goes from looking to staring and from staring to a plan of action. He finally approaches her and even though he's nervous, something tells him to go on and do it anyway. That something is the evil desires that are still hidden deep within him. He tells her some corny line like, you must be tired because you have been running around all day in my mind.

Wow, she thinks he's funny and very easy to talk to already as they both notice each other's wedding rings. Their marriage commitments and partner's roles come up very briefly in the conversation. They are having some difficulties in their marriages and they express their unhappiness with it. Neither is telling the whole truth about it because, believe it or not, they both have like spirits and like spirits have the tendency to attract one another. The conversation is going awesome; he eventually realizes that she is just what he has been looking for in a women all his life. He learns all of this and believes it to be true based on a brief two-hour conversation. He begins to set up the next opportunity for them to see one another. They're both overtaken by what they have shared in the conversation and for that brief moment in time they quickly forgot all about the ones they took vows with. The vows that they took before God and their family friends and loved ones are no longer important to either one of them. They both see a window of opportunity to have their needs met and gain the much desired attention that they both have been longing for. The two agree that everything happens for a reason and they believe this must be their chance at true happiness. They also believe that God has brought them together for such a time as this, to finally be happy in life based on the prayers that they have sent up about their current frustrated situations. They can no longer see the immoral decision that they are about to make concerning their family's well-being and way of life. See, like Apostle Paul's expression, "that every time I will to do good evil is ever present," they both now are faced

The Pain In Pleasure

with decisions that will change their lives forever. The changes could be natural as well as spiritual. Will they both be bound by the lust of their eyes, their actions, or will they seek divine deliverance before this thing gets out of control?

Here we have two professing Christians making decisions based on what is driving them, their flesh. The flesh will trick us into doing things that we will later regret. The scripture below will give a foundational base for understanding this example.

Ephesians 4:18-19, *"Their moral understanding is darkened and their reasoning is beclouded. [They are] alienated (estranged, self-banished) from the life of God [with no share in it; this is] because of the ignorance (the want of knowledge and perception, the willful blindness) that is deep-seated in them, due to their hardness of heart [to the insensitiveness of their moral nature]..."*

"In their spiritual apathy they have become callous and past feeling reckless and have abandoned themselves [a prey] to unbridled sensuality, eager and greedy to indulge in every form of impurity [that their depraved desires may suggest and demand." The Holy

scriptures express the impact of allowing my flesh to control my actions and the result of doing so.

The natural tendency of human beings is to think they're okay and that they are light years away from God, leaving them hopelessly confused. Intellectual pride, rationalizations, and excuses all keep people from God. Don't be surprised if people can't grasp the Good News. The Good News will seem foolish to those who forsake faith and rely on their own understanding. People should be able to see a difference between Christians and non-Christians because of the way Christ lives in us. We are to live full of His light. Living the Christian life is a process. Although we have been given a new nature, we don't automatically think all good thoughts and express all right attitudes when we become a new people in Christ. But if we keep listening to the Holy Spirit, we will be changing all the time from glory to glory. Look back over the last few years in your life; do you see a clear process of change for the better in your thoughts, attitudes, and actions? Although change maybe slow, it comes each day as we trust God to change us.

The Pain In Pleasure

Paul describes in Galatians 5:17, when you follow the desires of your sinful nature the results are very clear: sexual immorality, impurity, lustful pleasures, etc. Paul describes the many forces that are fighting within us, the Spirit of God and the sinful nature or our evil desires, and the inclinations that stem from our body. The forces are not equal. The Spirit of God is infinitely stronger than any force. If we rely on our own wisdom, we will make many wrong choices. If we try to follow the Spirit by our own human effort, we will also fail. Our only way to freedom from our evil desires is through the empowering of the Holy Spirit. We all have evil desires, and we can't afford to ignore them. These desires include obvious sins, such as sexual immorality and demonic activities. They also include less obvious sins such as hostility, jealousy, and selfish ambitions, and neither is limited to just what I mentioned.

In order to accept Christ as our Savior, we need to turn from our sins and willingly nail our sinful nature to the cross. This doesn't mean, however, that we will never see traces of its evil desires again. Even as born again believers, we still have so much evil inside of us that is still in need of being delivered from us. Some of the evil that we posses inside of us have yet to be revealed to us; because of this we feel that we are good and exempt from ever sinning again. The scriptures teach that all have sinned and come short of the glory of God. The scriptures further inform us that if any man says that he is without sin, then he is a liar and the truth isn't in him.

As God's children, we still have the capacity to sin but we are given the power to overcome. We have been set free from sin's power over us and no longer have to give in to it. We must daily commit our sinful tendencies to God's control. Daily we must crucify the flesh moment by moment, drawing totally on the Spirit of God to overcome evil. God is interested in every area of our lives, not just the spiritual part. As we live by the Holy Spirit's power, we must learn to submit every aspect of our lives to God: emotional, physical, social, intellectual, and vocational. The commitment to God, along with the working of the Holy Spirit, removes the pain or the pleasures that we were enslaved to. God also supplies every opportunity to educate all of us to learn of Him

The Pain In Pleasure

through His Holy Word and inspired men and women. God loves us so much that He gives warning after warning and no man knows the day of His final warning. Warning does come before destruction and God is no respecter of persons. Please review the following scriptures and take heed to this warning.

2 Peter 2 (Amplified Bible)

"BUT ALSO [in those days] there arose false prophets among the people, just as there will be false teachers among yourselves, who will subtly and stealthily introduce heretical doctrines (destructive heresies), even denying and disowning the Master Who bought them, bringing upon themselves swift destruction."

"And many will follow their immoral ways and lascivious doings; because of them the true Way will be maligned and defamed."

"And in their covetousness (lust, greed) they will exploit you with false (cunning) arguments. From of old the sentence [of condemnation] for them has not been idle; their destruction (eternal misery) has not been asleep."

"For God did not [even] spare angels that sinned, but cast them into hell, delivering them to be kept there in pits of gloom till the judgment and their doom."

It is my sincere hope and desires that these last two scriptures have both encouraged you and inspired you to change the way you think and do business from this day forth and forevermore. I believe the information that you have read will continue to feed your spirit each time you read it. I pray that the scriptures I have included will forever stand out in your heart and mind.

Ephesians 6:10-12 (Amplified Bible)

"In conclusion, be strong in the Lord [be empowered through your union with Him]; draw your strength from Him [that strength which His boundless might provides]."

"Put on God's whole armor [the armor of a heavy-armed soldier which God supplies], that you may be able successfully to stand up against [all] the strategies and the deceits of the devil."

"For we are not wrestling with flesh and blood [contending only with physical opponents], but against

the despotisms, against the powers, against [the master spirits who are] the world rulers of this present darkness, against the spirit forces of wickedness in the heavenly (supernatural) sphere."

2 Timothy 2:15-16 (Amplified Bible)

"Study and be eager and do your utmost to present yourself to God approved (tested by trial), a workman who has no cause to be ashamed, correctly analyzing and accurately dividing [rightly handling and skillfully teaching] the Word of Truth."

"But avoid all empty (vain, useless, idle) talk, for it will lead people into more and more ungodliness."

The power and purpose of the blood of Jesus empowers us to be more than conquers through Christ Jesus with the full understanding that I truly can do all things through Christ Jesus who strengthens me. There is no longer any analogy or excuse that we can use to remove the power in the purpose that God has for us or the power in the blood that strengthens us to overcome the pain in pleasure. I pray that this book has taken you on an emotional rollercoaster ride, turning you inside out and upside down to the point of sincere change. I pray the analogies and scriptures provoke the inner most parts of your spirit, and provide you with a new awakening to the world around you that you are now fully persuaded to follow after Christ. May God Bless the reader, hearer, and doer of His inspired word, to go fourth with all power and authority both in heaven and on earth.

The Pain In Pleasure

Scripture References

The Pain In Pleasure

Scripture References

Romans 12:1-3 (Amplified Bible)

"I APPEAL to you therefore, brethren, and beg of you in view of [all] the mercies of God, to make a decisive dedication of your bodies [presenting all your members and faculties] as a living sacrifice, holy (devoted, consecrated) and well pleasing to God, which is your reasonable (rational, intelligent) service and spiritual worship."

"Do not be conformed to this world (this age), [fashioned after and adapted to its external, superficial customs], but be transformed (changed) by the [entire] renewal of your mind [by its new ideals and its new attitude], so that you may prove [for yourselves] what is the good and acceptable and perfect will of God, even the thing which is good and acceptable and perfect [in His sight for you]."

"For by the grace (unmerited favor of God) given to me I warn everyone among you not to estimate and think of himself more highly than he ought [not to have an **exaggerated opinion of his own importance**], but to rate his ability with sober judgment, each according to the degree of faith apportioned by God to him."

Psalm 24 7-10

"Lift up your heads, O you gates; and be lifted up, you age-abiding doors, that the King of glory may come in."

"Who is the King of glory? The Lord strong and mighty, the Lord mighty in battle."

"Lift up your heads, O you gates; yes, lift them up, you age-abiding doors that the King of glory may come in."

"Who is [He then] this King of glory? The Lord of hosts, He is the King of glory. Selah [pause, and think of that]!"

Psalm 111:1-10 (Amplified Bible)

"PRAISE THE Lord! (Hallelujah!) I will praise and give thanks to the Lord with my whole heart in the council of the upright and in the congregation." The works of the Lord are great, sought out by all those who have delight in them."

"His work is honorable and glorious, and His righteousness endures forever. He has made His wonderful works to be remembered; the Lord is gracious, merciful, and full of loving compassion. He has given food and provision to those who reverently and worshipfully fear Him; He will remember His covenant forever and imprint it [on His

The Pain In Pleasure

mind]. He has declared and shown to His people the power of His works in giving them the heritage of the nations [of Canaan]."

"The works of His hands are [absolute] truth and justice [faithful and right]; and all His decrees and precepts are sure (fixed, established, and trustworthy). They stand fast and are established forever and ever and are done in [absolute] truth and uprightness."

"He has sent redemption to His people; He has commanded His covenant to be forever; holy is His name, inspiring awe, reverence, and godly fear."

"The reverent fear and worship of the Lord is the beginning of wisdom and skill [the preceding and the first essential, the prerequisite and the alphabet]; a good understanding, wisdom, and meaning have all those who do [the will of the Lord]. Their praise of Him endures forever."

Isaiah 40:31 *"But they that wait upon the Lord shall renew their strength; they shall mount up with wings as eagles; they shall run, and not be weary, and they shall walk and not faint."* NOTE - The word "wait" in this *verse implies a positive action of hope, based on knowing that the Word of God is a true fact and that it will soon come to pass - waiting with earnest expectation!*

Psalm 34:19 *"Many are the afflictions of the righteous, but the LORD delivers him out of them all."*

Jeremiah 30:17 *"For I will restore health unto you, and I will heal you of your wounds, saith the Lord."*

Jeremiah 33:6 *"Behold, I will bring you health and cure, and I will cure you, and will reveal unto you the abundance of peace and truth."*

Matthew 18:19 *"Again I say to you that if two of you agree on Earth concerning anything that they ask, it will be done for them by My Father in heaven." NOTE - The prayer of agreement is powerful - have someone agree with you for your healing!"*

Mark 11:24 *"Therefore I say to you whatever things you ask when you pray, believe that you receive them, and you will have them." Surely this includes healing!"*

The Pain In Pleasure

Isaiah 58:8 *"Thy light shall break forth as the morning, and thy health shall spring forth speedily; and thy righteousness shall go before thee: the glory of the Lord shall be thy rear guard."*

Thessalonians 5:23 *"And the very God of peace sanctify you wholly [completely]; and I pray God your whole spirit and soul and body be preserved blameless [sound, complete and intact] unto the coming of our Lord Jesus Christ."*

NOTE - It is very clear in this passage that wholeness, wellness, and health are for the complete make-up of man, spiritual, mental, and physical.

1 Peter 2:24 *"Who Himself bore our sins in His own body on the tree, that we, having died to sins, might live for righteousness--by whose stripes you were healed."*
NOTE - Past tense *"You were healed"*. Jesus paid it all for your total deliverance - spirit, soul and body!

Psalm 103:2-3 *"Bless the Lord, O my soul, and forget not all His benefits: Who forgiveth all thine niquities; who heals all thy diseases"*

NOTE - Notice it doesn't say some, it says all! It also states that healing is one of the benefits that belong to the believer along with the benefit of having our sin forgiven. See our article **Two Gifts of Grace**.

3 John 2 *"Beloved, I wish above all things that thou mayest prosper and be in health, even as thy soul prospereth."*

Jeremiah 17:14 *"Heal me, O LORD, and I shall be healed; save me, and I shall be saved: for thou art my praise."*

NOTE - Once a person finally understands that healing is a part of the finished work of grace along with salvation, paid for at the same time with the same healing Blood, then you can get excited about this verse saying; "You did it Lord for me! Then according to this verse I will agree and say, *I will have healing just as I have salvation*, it's mine NOW!"

James 5:14-15 *"Is any sick among you? Let him call for the elders of the church; and let them pray over him, anointing him with oil in the name of the Lord: And the prayer of faith shall save the sick, and the Lord shall raise him up;*

and if he have committed sins, they shall be forgiven him."

1 Thessalonians 5:8-10 8 *"But let us who are of the day [in Christ] be sober [Word minded], putting on the breastplate of faith and love, and as a helmet the hope of salvation. For God did not appoint us to wrath [the curse], but to obtain salvation through our Lord Jesus Christ, who died for us, that whether we wake or sleep, we should live together with Him [share in His life]."*

NOTE - While this block of Scripture is talking about end times and the rapture of the Church, it is important not to miss the heart of God toward us the Church, which is constant and never changing. The curse does not belong to us, we were not appointed to it, we are appointed to the blessing which is the life of Christ given to us. The Word salvation always implies healing, mending, health as well as deliverance. One should always translate the word salvation as saved-healed! Don't miss this great truth, the Lord wants you to obtain healing, both now and in the glorious completeness of it when we go to be with Him.

Scriptures to Build Confidence

Isaiah 54:17 *"No weapon formed against you shall prosper, and every tongue which rises against you in judgment YOU shall condemn. This is the heritage (birthright) of the servants of the LORD, and their righteousness is from Me," says the LORD." NOTE - Sickness is judging you falsely, it's your birthright to live in health. You condemn it, with the Word of God, and command it to leave your body.*

Matthew 18:18 *"Verily I say unto you, whatsoever you shall bind on earth shall be bound in heaven: and whatsoever you shall loose on earth shall be loosed in heaven."*

NOTE - The word "bind" means to forbid, the word "loose" means to let go or to allow to go free. Do not allow sickness, pain or disease run free in your body, bind it or forbid it to stay there any longer because of your rights as a believer.. Put your foot down and command it to leave in the Name of Jesus!!!

The Pain In Pleasure

John 10:10 *"The thief (satan) does not come except to steal, and to kill, and to destroy. I (Jesus) have come that they may have life, and that they may have it more abundantly."*

NOTE - Here we see the desired will of the Lord for every believer - *that we experience abundant life.* According to this verse He came for this very purpose. We also see clearly that it is not God who afflicts us. The word here for *life* is the Greek word "zoe." One highly respected commentator describes the true meaning of the word *life* in this verse as: "life being the highest and best of which Christ is." In light of that meaning, you can easily see the wonderful gift of life the Lord wants for each of us. Sickness and disease are truly not in His plan for us, simply because He has none to give.

Luke 10:19 *"Behold, I give unto you power (authority) to tread on serpents and scorpions, and over all the power of the enemy: and nothing shall by any means hurt you."*

NOTE - This is an exciting verse as Jesus said He has given us authoritative power over ALL, not some of the enemy!

Command Satan to take his hands off of you. Command sickness and disease to leave you now in the Name of Jesus.

Isaiah 41:10 *"So do not fear, for I am with you; do not be dismayed, for I am your God. I will strengthen you and help you; I will uphold you with my righteous right hand."*

John 4:4 *".... greater is he that is in you, than he that is in the world."*

1 John 5:4 *"For whatsoever is born of God overcometh the world: and this is the victory that overcometh the world, even our faith."*

NOTE - In John 17:14 Jesus states that we as believer's are not of the world. Sickness, disease and failure belong to the world. As a believer, we are given the right to overcome that which comes against us by holding fast to the Word of God. While we do not deny that the problem or circumstance exists, we do however deny it the right to stay through our faith in God and His Word!!! Know this: Faith in God is victory all of the time!!!

Romans 8:31 *"What shall we then say to these things? If God be for us, who can be against us"*

The Pain In Pleasure

NOTE - You are a winner, you are victorious through the Lord Jesus Christ. Begin to see yourself the way God sees you.

1 John 4:17 *"Love has been perfected among us in this: that we may have boldness in the day of judgment; because as He is, so are we in this world."*

NOTE - Not only can we have boldness in the day of judgment, but we can have boldness now in this life, in the face of adversity, knowing who we are in Christ, knowing what belongs to us in Him and tenaciously holding onto it, refusing what the enemy wants us to have. As this verse says so clearly, as He is, so are we in this world. Think about that for a moment, how is He now? He is not sick, He is not diseased - it can't touch Him, and we are His body - the body of Christ. Insist on having the blessing of the Lord manifested in you - praise Him for it now, worship Him!!!

Jeremiah 29:11 *"For I know the thoughts that I think toward you, says the Lord, thoughts of peace and not of evil, to give you a future and a hope (an expected end)."*

NOTE - Again, the word for peace here in the Hebrew is the word *shalom* and implies the meaning of health and prosperity, which is obviously His will as it is the end or goal that the Lord is expecting for us. Begin to expect it - yes, that's right - get your hopes way up!

2 Timothy 3:2 *"People will be lovers of themselves, lovers of money, boastful, proud, abusive, disobedient to their parents, ungrateful, unholy."*

The Pain In Pleasure

Lawrence V. Bolar

ABOUT THE AUTHOR

Lawrence Bolar was born in Picayune, Mississippi. He graduated from Picayune Memorial High School; and attended Pearl River Community College where he received an Associate Degree. Lawrence transferred to Virginia State University where he received a Bachelor of Science degree in 1996 and a Master of Education in Counseling in 1999. He also earned an endorsement in Administration & Supervision from Virginia State University in 2004.

Lawrence has been in the field of education for the last 15 years. He is currently working as a high school assistant principal. Lawrence has worked in various localities as a high school and middle school counselor in private and public schools, as well as the Department of Correctional Education. As well, he serves as a community counselor and program director for various agencies providing services for juvenile and adult clients living in group homes through mental health and social services.

Lawrence Bolar is the published author of two books: **"Nothing Substitutes Time"** an inspirational and though provoking book that educates and empowers the importance of building strong family relationships with a special emphasis on the role of the Father. **"Summers with Lauren"** his second book is the first of a five series children's book that shares the adventures of a little boy named Christian who attempts to manipulate his dad to stay up. In turn, his dad manipulates him to learn how to pray by reading him a story about Lauren, a little girl who gets to spend her very first summer with her dad and many challenges occur. Lawrence's Bolar's third book, due to be released next month, is called, " The Pain In Pleasure" another inspirational, thought-provoking book filled with relevant analogies about how the pleasures we experience in life may have hidden pain attached to them that not only affects us but all the people who love us.

Lawrence Bolar diligently serves as an active Christian educator, licensed and ordained minister, and a mentor/educator in the schools and the community.

OTHER PRODUCTS BY LAWRENCE BOLAR

Nothing Substitutes Time

Summers With Lauren

To order additional copies, post comments, or schedule an author visit, please forward your requests to:

Lawrence Bolar
c/o The Pain in Pleasure
P.O. Box 1021, Sandston, VA 23150
(E-mail): Lawrence@lawrencebolar.com
(Website): www.lawrencebolar.com

Qty.	Item	Unit Cost	Total
	The Pain in Pleasure	$16.00	
	In Virginia add 5% sales tax	Subtotal	
		Shipping	
		Grand Total	

SHIPPING & HANDLING: Please add $3.00 shipping for each item For orders placed outside of the U.S., add $6.00 shipping per item.

Ship to: Organization: _____

_____   _____ (Mr./Mrs./Ms.)_____
Last Name   First Name

_____
Street Address

_____, _____   _____
City   State   Zip

Phone: (   ) _____   E-mail:_____

THANK YOU FOR PLACING YOUR ORDER!!!